Try not to be a cunt using my ideas. And if you have to be, try not to be a very big one.

Art of Grey Area Thinking

Helping Young People Fight Extremism, Manipulation, and Abuse

By Jimmy from The Good Fight

Hey Maya!

Thanks for reading my book! Rachel from USC Hillel told me you went to be a screenwriter! It's awesome to be sharing Grey Area Thinking with a fellow writer!

Copyright

Author's disclaimer: I, the author, put my heart and soul into this book. On this topic, my readers must get my absolute best. Therefore, I tormented myself over every idea, suggestion, and insight in this book. However, it's just a book intended for education and the sharing of ideas.

I am NOT providing professional advice or services to the reader. My writing is NOT intended to be a substitute for seeking professional guidance. I cannot be held liable or responsible for any loss or damage allegedly arising from any suggestion or information contained in this book. If you a victim of abuse, please contact the authorities and seek professional help immediately. And if you are an abusive person who got your ass kicked by one of my readers, sucks to suck. You still can't sue me.

Memoir disclaimer: This work depicts actual events in the life of the author as truthfully as recollection permits. While all persons within are actual individuals, names and identifying characteristics have been changed to respect their privacy. There are a few exceptions.

Dedicated To:

Cyrus
The Women of Iran
The People of Ukraine
The Yazidi People

Acknowledgments

Edited by: Aby Richards from AJR Editing.

Note: For stylistic purposes, I made intentional grammatical errors and told Aby not to change them.

Front cover designed by: Ulyana Dikhtyar. Ulyana is a young girl who currently resides in Kharkiv, Ukraine. At the time of her work, the Russian front line was only several miles away. Ulyana completed the task while facing daily Russian bombardments and frequent blackouts. Ulyana's father Yuri also helped facilitate the design process.

Book illustrations drawn by: Soloviov Dymtro, Ulyana Dikhtyar, and Nadif Abdelhak.

Special thanks to each and every one of my twenty-one beta readers, including the harshest critics. This book would not be what it is without you guys.

Special thanks to my consultant Jennifer Singer.

Special thanks to Michael La Ronn's Youtube Channel: Author Level Up, which provided valuable insight to help me self-publish my first book.

Table of Contents

Tactical Table of Contents

Your understanding of these tactics and strategies may be less effective if you do not read the entire book first.

Welcome to the Art of Grey Area Thinking

What The Heck Is This?

What is this book?

The Art of Grey Area Thinking is a mental martial art I created to help young people achieve victory against abusive manipulation and extremism.

What is victory?

Victory means "problem solved." That can mean different things. It can be something as simple as walking away from an asshole and never looking back. It can also be something as ambitious as taking down a regime state's propaganda machine.

Grey area thinking is about finding unique solutions to unique problems.

How do I plan to help?

I teach readers how to fight because that is what I know best. My speciality is identifying abuse tactics and coming up with countermeasures.

Furthermore, I teach people how to stop the spread of extremism by dismantling the manipulative arguments that form the foundations of extreme ideologies.

The Bigger Picture

Before I explain what grey area thinking is, I want to explain the bigger picture. The purpose of my book isn't to teach you how to argue or dominate people.

You will definitely learn how to fight, but I hope you avoid it as much as possible. Like in real life, the true value of learning martial arts isn't your ability to beat people up. Rather, it's the life lessons you learn studying the art.

The focus of this book is mental, emotional, and social combat. But I want to take you beyond that. I want to connect you to larger life lessons.

My ultimate purpose is to teach you the Art of Grey Area Thinking. The tactics and strategies I teach cannot be divorced from the mindset of grey area thinking.

The world doesn't need more people who only know how to fight. It needs people who can effectively navigate and build in an increasingly complex and ambiguous world. The Art of Grey Area Thinking is a journey that helps you do both.

What Is Grey Area Thinking

The Journey of a Grey Area Thinker

1.) Become a more versatile and precise problem solver

2.) Develop a supple mind that can see what is not obvious

3.) Overcome manipulation and psychological abuse

4.) Overcome the influence of extremists

What is Grey Area Thinking?

Grey area thinking is a term commonly used to:

1.) Criticize the problems created by toxic black-and-white thinking

2.) Encourage people to see nuance and uniqueness in different people and situations rather than overgeneralizing

3.) Make people realize that there are exceptions to established rules and beliefs

4.) Prevent people who are experiencing emotional pain from developing destructive black-and-white beliefs

5.) Help people understand complex political and social issues

Grey area thinking is open to interpretation. I do not own the term. The following definition is my interpretation:

Grey area thinking is striving to do the right thing, in the right way, at the right time, in the right amount, for the right reasons, and with respect to our limits.

"With respect to our limits" is key. Few things would get done if we refused to act until the first five conditions were perfect. Grey area thinking is not about perfection.

It's about the lifelong journey of exploration, engagement, reflection, adjustment, and growth. It's about becoming a more <u>precise</u> thinker over time. It's about building a supple mind that is <u>flexible</u> but unbreakable.

Grey area thinkers are <u>versatile</u> problem solvers who can approach problems from different angles and spot non-obvious solutions. The grey area thinker considers the <u>bigger picture</u> and the <u>long term</u>.

What Is Black-And-White Thinking?

What Is Black-and-White Thinking?

"Black-and-white thinking" is what cool people say to criticize absolute thinking, which, put simply, is "this is the only way."

Is Black-and-White Thinking Always Bad?

Of course not! Is it unreasonable for a boss to say, "I will always fire someone who never shows up to work?"

Besides, to say "black and white is always bad" is in itself a fallacious black-and-white statement.

If we walk around telling everyone black-and-white thinking is bad, it would be pretty damn easy for people to find something we said that is black-and-white and call us a hypocrite.

In fact you may see me sometimes speak in absolutes in this very book. I try not to, but I'm human.

Grey area thinking is not the sworn enemy of black-and-white thinking. But when black-and-white thinking becomes a problem, grey area thinkers take it down.

When Does Black-And-White Thinking Become A Problem?

Black-and-white thinking becomes a problem when it is used in a harmful manner.

For example, an abusive partner who says to their lover, "You're nothing without me." Or the self-abusing lover who says, "I am nothing without my partner."

Another example is the cult leader who says, "I alone have all the answers. The lifestyle I practice is the only worthy lifestyle. You can only live this worthy lifestyle by abandoning everything and following me."

Religious fanatics who encourage violence against those who do not follow their religion are people who practice black-and-white thinking in its most dangerous and abusive form.

The common denominator of problematic black-and-white thinking is that force, pressure, deceit, and ignorance are used to make people believe in a false absolute.

Reader Expectations

What Is This Book Not?

Not a philosophy. Grey Area Thinking is a mindset. Nor am I here to argue absolutism vs. relativism.

Not a persuasive piece. I'm not here to persuade people not to be abusive, manipulative, or extreme. I'm here to help people kick their asses.

Not an academic paper. I'm not citing research. I know this is important for many intellectuals, but it kills the flow of my writing. If I get something wrong, listen to the fact-checkers.

Is the Art of Grey Area Thinking For Everyone?

Nope.

According to one beta reader, the people who "need this book the most" will probably want to "tear it apart afterwards."

If someone is already an extremist or an abusive manipulator, reading this book won't help them. They will get triggered. They will get angry. Being nice doesn't matter. So I won't bother.

I'm not calling anyone a lost cause. I'm not saying they don't deserve compassion or help. I'm saying that my focus in this book is to help people who struggle against them.

I encourage you to adapt grey area thinking for persuasion. But in this book, I won't try to persuade anyone.

I'd rather help the readers who don't need to be persuaded. The more I need to persuade, the more I have to explain. The more I have to explain, the more those who don't need explanations will get bored.

To my intended readers, I hope to give you tools you can use to overcome manipulation, toxic beliefs, extreme rhetoric, and fallacious arguments. You will be a voice of reason to people vulnerable to those things.

Who Is It For?

So... Who Is It For?

For the women of Iran, who are beaten, raped, and killed by religious fanatics. So the world can help them overthrow their regime and create a society where it never happens again.

For Ukrainians who call their relatives in Russia to inform them about dead family and are told, "then why did your country start the war?" So they can fight the Russian propaganda machine that crosses any line it can.

For anyone dealing with current abuse and trying to process past abuse. So they can give themselves closure, emerge stronger, and defeat anyone foolish enough to try it again.

For young people who have friends and family on the fence about joining cults, pyramid schemes, or extreme movements. So they can intervene before it is too late.

For moderates who have been bullied into submission by extremists, so when their extremists give them the usual ultimatum, "with us or against the cause," the moderates can finally say, "against you FOR the cause."

While I did not intend this to be a mental health book, some beta readers remarked that reading this book could have mental health benefits. One reader said she felt "empowered." Another said that she could see it being "useful to therapists who treat anxiety."

So, this book is also for anyone who would find it therapeutic.

Art And Grey Area Thinking

How Will I Teach Grey Area Thinking?

I will teach the Art of Grey Thinking using universal art principles. The principles are: balance, contrast, emphasis, scale, variety, unity, direction, and performance. I do this for several reasons.

First, art changes the way we feel. Human emotions are stronger than human logic. Art encompasses human emotions in a way logic does not and, therefore, can teach values logic cannot.

Second, principles are easier to remember. During a heated conflict, we need a reliable way to organize our thoughts.

Third, principles allow you to innovate. I want my readers to be able to create their own solutions rather than rely on scripts I give them.

Fourth, principles allow evolution. Abusive manipulators are constantly adapting and evolving their tactics. Nothing is stopping a narcissistic sociopath from picking up my book and figuring out how to beat specific strategies.

Furthermore, corrupt people can hijack ideas. Manipulators twist words. My writing can be exploited in ways that my beta readers, editor, and I cannot predict at this time.

Therefore, I must give my readers a flexible set of principles so they can evolve alongside the threat and develop their own strategies as the times change.

The Elements Beyond Principles

While most art shares the same principles, each art has its own unique elements. Painting has its lines and colors. Film has its sound and acting. Martial arts has its striking and grappling.

As a mental art, grey area elements are the thinker's mental qualities, such as emotional intelligence and character. Elements will be explained after the principles.

My Art

Art is about expression. As the artist, I'm going to express myself fully. While I won't tell the reader what to think, I won't hide my bias. I won't pretend not to be there.

The Principles

The eight principles are: balance, contrast, emphasis, scale, variety, unity, direction, and performance. These principles are abstract. To use them, we have to turn them into something real.

I will show you how I interpret these principles. I will show you how I analyze problems with these principles. Finally, I will show you how I turn these principles into strategies to attack abusive manipulation and extremism.

Ultimately, I want my readers to develop their own skills to interpret, analyze, and solve problems using these principles.

The principles work together; one problem can be analyzed using multiple principles. This section will explain each principle individually. Ultimately, they can overlap and intertwine to solve more complex issues.

Principle One: Balance

Balance is a continuous search for more precise boundaries.

Feeling The Principle: Balance

Balance is essential in many fields: health, yoga, architecture, juggling, and more. Regardless of the field, balance means optimal and sustainable function.

In other words, all needs are met, and all threats are removed. To do that, you need boundaries. Boundaries can take on many different forms.

Today, "boundaries" is a term commonly used to establish a code of conduct in relationships. However, I believe that boundaries exist whenever balance is involved.

For good health, balance means setting boundaries against unhealthy foods, habits, and environments. Healthy choices also require boundaries. Those boundaries take the shape of habits, discipline, commitment, and self-control. Balanced health is achieved by meeting those boundaries.

In architecture, balance means symmetry and stability. Thus, boundaries take the shape of measurements, blueprints, layouts, and city building codes. Buildings in earthquake zones must be able to withstand future threats. Hence, boundaries must encompass mandatory earthquake-proof materials and construction.

An artistic gymnast doing a handstand has to activate multiple groups of muscles in the arms, shoulders, back, core, butt, and legs. However, gymnasts can't just flex every muscle as hard as possible, as the handstand would collapse.

The gymnast must intuit how much activation each muscle group requires. Some require full contraction, while others need a softer touch. Flex one group of muscles too hard, and the gymnast loses balance. Therefore, each muscle group must activate to a minimum boundary but not past a maximum boundary.

Gymnastic coaches will sometimes test a gymnast's resilience by pushing them while they are in handstand. To maintain the handstand, the gymnast must quickly make the correct adjustments.

With more practice, the gymnast's muscular control becomes more and more precise, leading to a more perfectly-balanced handstand. Thus, the gymnast is continuously searching for more precise boundaries.

In all fields, the search for more precise boundaries is a continuous process. With more precise boundaries, more needs are met, and the balance lasts longer.

Artist: Soloviov Dymtro

What Does Balance Have to Do with Grey Area Thinking?

Grey area thinkers who master balance are excellent problem solvers. How do you achieve balance? Meet needs. Clear obstacles. Create boundaries to protect your needs. Improve boundaries to meet more needs. Sounds like problem-solving.

Grey area thinkers must *keep the focus on needs*. We don't just use grey area thinking for the sake of the grey area. Without balance, grey area thinking loses its meaning.

For example, someone who is bleeding out has to either get medical attention or die. It may be black-and-white thinking, but that's what's needed in this situation. Grey area thinkers would be ridiculous to criticize reasonable uses of black-and-white thinking.

Grey area thinking is about doing the right thing, in the right way, for the right reasons, at the right time, in the right amount, with respect to our limits. Sometimes, black-and-white is the right thing.

This might sound contradictory, but when it is reasonable, black-and-white thinking is part of grey area thinking.

We only criticize black-and-white thinking when it becomes the problem. Otherwise, grey area thinking encompasses reasonable black-and-white thinking.

Your Workspace

This space is for you. Do whatever you want with it. Sometimes, I give you prompts, but most of the time, I don't.

Author's Comments: Balanced Choioos

The final part of this book will be a memoir explaining who I am, why I wrote this book, and why I'm qualified to speak on this subject. I know nonfiction authors are expected to declare their qualifications upfront, but I have chosen to do the opposite.

I feel my qualifications are best explained by stories, and those stories are best told at the end. In the meantime, you will see my personal commentary throughout this book.

As the author, the nine words, "Balance is a continuous search for more precise boundaries," will always be the longest part of this book because it took me many years to truly understand what balance is.

I used to think like most people: that balance is two equal parts of two opposite things. Then, in 2016, I got really sick. For weeks, I woke up laughing hysterically. By noon, I was crying hysterically. Then laughing again. The cycle repeated itself all day, every day. Two opposite actions in equal proportion. If that is "balance," then I wouldn't wish balance upon Hitler.

Equality and balance are two different things. Balance must be defined by purpose rather than adjectives. Otherwise, balance would lose meaning. For example, if you broke your left leg, you restore balance by healing your left leg. You don't restore balance by shooting yourself in the right leg.

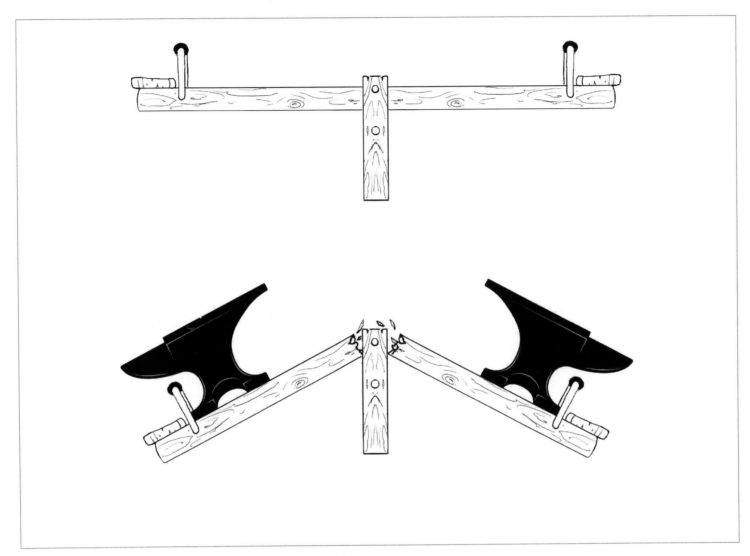

Artist: Soloviov Dymtro

When Does Black-and-White Thinking Become an Obstacle and Cause Imbalance?

We lose balance when we push one need past its boundaries, and it interferes with other needs. The cancerous need demands more attention than it truly requires, causing us to neglect other needs.

A common way this happens is when people go too far for success. It is the workaholic who neglects their health and family. It is the corporation that destroys the environment and harms public health. It is the business that exploits workers and has no social responsibility.

In the long run, neglected needs have consequences. Sometimes, those consequences are so severe, they erase all gains made from attending to a favorite need.

For example, if a parent uses extreme methods to make their children successful, their child may grow up to become mentally unstable, socially inept, or morally bankrupt. Any one of those consequences has the potential to ultimately destroy any success obtained.

Your Workspace

25

Grey Area Structure

"Grey Area Structure" is a section where I use imagery to help Grey Area Thinkers organize their thoughts.

In the structure above, the triangle fills a need. However, because it exceeds its boundaries, it has become an obstacle for the structure's completion.

Why is Balance a Continuous Search?

In life, balance is not perfect. However, people normally don't care if things are 'good enough'. That is until a stressful event occurs, and suddenly 'good enough' is no longer good enough.

Consider the scenario where a small city of 500,000 habitants suddenly receives 50,000 refugees. The city's government, infrastructure, and residents will be severely challenged. Problems that people tolerated before (such as poor sanitation) may suddenly become intolerable.

Citizens may initially welcome refugees, but if their lives are constantly disrupted, they may turn hostile. Sympathetic people may temporarily put aside needs such as stability and security; however, sympathy will run dry if those needs are constantly neglected. Therefore, compassion must be balanced with safety, stability, and security needs.

Because change is constant, loss of balance is inevitable. Unexpected trouble tests our boundaries. They reveal weaknesses we never had to fix before. This forces us to improve those boundaries to better meet future challenges.

Grey Area Structure

"Grey Area Structure" is a section where I use imagery to help Grey Area Thinkers organize their thoughts.

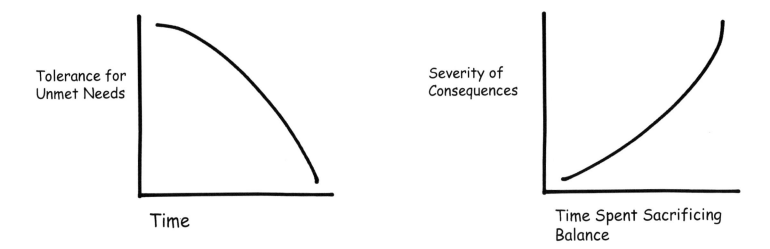

What is the Relationship Between Extremism and Balance?

Each need requires space to flourish. Extremists severely overestimate the amount of space their favorite needs demand. So they invade space required by other needs to make room for theirs.

One group of extremists may inspire people to join the opposite extreme. This creates political polarization, forcing people to pick a side dominated by extremists.

It is common to hear polarizing activists say, "Join our extreme social justice movement, or you are part of the problem." This statement pressures people who care about social justice to submit to the extreme narrative. Additionally, neutral people who hear that statement may become angry and join the opposition out of spite.

In this scenario, the need for social justice threatens people's need for autonomy. People feel violated, so they may join opposite extremes or become apathetic. Thus, ironically, extreme social justice becomes an obstacle to social justice itself.

In the end, polarization is a destructive stalemate that wreaks havoc on society's balance. No one's needs are getting met.

How Can the Principle of Balance Be Used to Fight Against Manipulation and Abuse?

In martial arts, fighters must maintain balance at all times while attacking, defending, and moving. A physical fight has many of the same dynamics as a mental fight. Fighters and manipulators both seek control.

Manipulators aim to control what they have no right to control. So you must know what belongs to you and maintain control over what's yours. Just like a fighter, maintain your inner balance.

For example, let's say a toxic self-help person says to you, "You're not [good enough]. This is why you're not [good enough]. I can make you [good enough]. If you don't listen to me, you're a loser."

What are they trying to control? Your destiny. Your beliefs. Your sense of self-worth. Your autonomy. Your insecurities. Those needs belong to YOU. And if you don't protect those needs with solid boundaries, then you give away control of your inner balance.

"My life belongs to me. My flaws belong to me. Maybe I am not [good enough], but that's my business. Want to touch what's mine? You ask for MY permission; my beliefs belong to me. Want to influence my beliefs? You influence on MY terms. Want to take what's mine? My permission is no; my terms are leave."

Your Workspace

30

How Do I Form Boundaries Against Bullies?

With boldness. Bullies prefer timid targets. Often, a bold spirit alone is enough to deter bullies.

Timid people are hesitant to set boundaries. They let bullies establish too much control before they draw the line. Let's look at a common bullying tactic called "moving the goalpost."

This happens when a powerful bully controls something the target needs. The need could be something real, like a job, or something abstract, like approval. The bully promises to provide that need if the target fills a requirement. However, when the requirement is filled, the bully says, "That's not enough; here's another requirement."

The bully is using the target's needs against them. "How far can I go to control this person? Can I get the target to destroy their own dignity? Can I get the target to destroy their own balance?"

Boldness denies bullies' control. It helps us form strong boundaries. It gives us the self-respect to walk away from toxic people. It allows us to go on the offense against the bully.

Even in situations where the bully is overwhelmingly powerful, boldness can limit the amount of control they are able to take. At the very least, boldness allows us to keep our dignity intact.

Your Workspace

How can the principle of balance help us overcome other common bullying tactics?

What About Manipulators Who Try to be Our Friends First?

Aggressive boundaries work against antagonistic manipulators, such as bullies or scam artists. But some manipulators are indirect and subtle. Often, they come to us as friends.

In the movie Star Wars Episode III: Revenge of the Sith, the evil Sith lord, Chancellor Palpatine, slowly manipulates the Jedi hero, Anakin Skywalker, into becoming the villain, Darth Vader. Posing as a friend, Palpatine subtly stokes Anakin's fears about his wife dying and his frustrations with his Jedi colleagues. Ultimately, the small manipulations lead Anakin to an absolute proposal: if you want your wife to live, join me. Betray the Jedi, and kill them all.

In real life, abusive narcissists use friendships as a way to gather information. A common tactic is to ask abnormally-high volumes of probing questions. Many people ask lots of personal questions when they start new friendships. However, with narcissist manipulators, it's non-stop probing. They want *everything as soon as possible*. Not only does this give them information to later use against the target, but it also tricks the target's mind into a false sense of familiarity.

Experienced manipulators progressively work their way in. This is why walls are not good boundaries. Walls don't protect specific needs. They are just generic obstacles to stop people from entering. A skillful manipulator can get around it or slowly dig their way in. Once in, there's a timid target waiting for them. Easy prey.

So how do we set boundaries against skillful, friendly, and subtle manipulators? *By continuously searching for more precise boundaries within ourselves.*

We cannot avoid contact with skillful manipulators. But the more we improve our inner balance, the harder it is for them to gain control.

Your wife or husband's life is important. But they are not so important that you throw away your humanity. We have a right to be upset if our colleagues don't respect us. But we can't just murder them. (Except Steve. You can murder Steve.)

Being polite is important, but not more important than your privacy. Don't let the need to be liked stop you from putting your foot down when a friendly person makes you uncomfortable.

When I feel like I'm being probed, I respond, "Why do you need to know?" or "Every additional question will cost you a dollar."

Your Workspace

What About Straight-Up Deception?

Deception attacks the target's sense of reality. If our reality is distorted, we won't understand what we need.

Abusive lovers gaslight their victims to lose trust in their own memory. When narcissistic abusers are about to be exposed, they brazenly play the victim and accuse others of their own flaws. Political mal-actors fire-hose misinformation to overwhelm fact-checkers.

The solution to dealing with reality distorters is to go on the offense. Defense is a losing game because there are endless ways to distort reality. So if you cannot walk away, attack. Threaten *their* balance. Attack *their* needs.

Similar to how cheating students face expulsion, reality distorters need to be threatened with something they care about. When people have to worry about their own balance, they have less energy to threaten yours.

Let's apply this principle to a common gaslighting strategy abusive people use.

When abusive people are confronted with their past behavior, they may suddenly pretend to be someone who is too nice for that kind of behavior. The gaslighter denies the behavior while instilling doubt within and against the accuser.

If the victim gets upset, the abuser can then say, "See, I'm the real victim here!"

The solution is to destroy the gaslighter's ability to maneuver. You force the gaslighter into a situation where they are trapped into playing their fake character... forever.

Say to the gaslighter, "Obviously, it's your word against mine. If you are so confident in your word, will you allow me to record a video of you denying your actions? In fact, in the future, any interaction between you and me should be recorded. That way, you can prove to the world what a liar I am."

If the gaslighter agrees, then the video creates a standard they must live up to (and will likely fail to do so). Even if the gaslighter refuses, you will still make them feel off-balanced and hesitant to target you in the future.

Your Workspace

In the 2022 Iran Woman-Freedom-Life revolution, Iranian regime cyber teams would pretend to be on the protester's side and spread negative news about the regime. Then, a few days later, they would debunk the story. This tactic is meant to demoralize and disrupt the protesters. The tactic instills distrust amongst protesters and creates an atmosphere of unpredictability and fear.

I dare not advise brave Iranians on how to fight a tyrannical regime. What can the world do to help brave Iranian protesters get trustworthy information?

What Is a Common Misconception About Balance?

The middle ground fallacy is the illusion that just because something is in the middle means it is balanced. This is not true. Balance is about meeting needs to create optimal functionality. If being in the middle of something leads to that, it's balance. Otherwise, middleness has nothing to do with balance.

Deep Dive: Compassion Is A Finite Resource

"The Last Lion" is a documentary about a single mother lioness who struggles to raise her cubs alone. The story starts with a small lion family: a lioness, a lion, and their three cubs. One day, a rival male invades, kills the father, and conquers their territory. When male lions conquer a territory, they kill the cubs and claim the lionesses.

Out of love for her children, the lioness took her cubs and left. She would raise them herself out in the wild. A month later, things were going badly. A crocodile killed one cub, and the other two were missing.

The lioness searched for days and finally found one cub. It was alive, but its back had been broken when it tried to play with a wild pig (damn it, Pumbaa). Nevertheless, the paraplegic cub was ecstatic to see its mother and army-crawled toward her as fast as it could. The lioness, an extremely affectionate and dedicated mother, took a very long look at her cub. Then, she turned around and ran.

Compassion is a finite resource. The lioness loved her child but understood that raising it was a lost cause. If she had tried, the effort could have cost her the opportunity to save her final cub.

Why is this important? Because balance isn't always fun. When we have to fulfill needs with limited resources, we must prioritize. Sometimes, balance requires us to sacrifice a need. After all, needs follow a hierarchy.

In November 2021, 28-year-old Nadia Murad, a survivor of the ISIS-Yazidi genocide and Nobel Peace Prize winner, was set to speak at a school in Toronto, Canada. However, the event was canceled by the school district's superintendent out of fear that it would promote Islamophobia and make students uncomfortable.

Murad, who spent months enduring horrific sexual violence after being kidnapped by ISIS, was silenced and humiliated. To the school district, her courageous story mattered less than student comfort.

Spending compassion on people who are too easily offended is like drinking seawater to quench thirst. It encourages more and more self-importance and fragility. Ultimately, it takes empathy away from people who really need it. People like to think they have unlimited compassion, but Toronto's treatment of Murad is why we need to prioritize compassion.

Shouldn't compassion be given to a genocide survivor before first-world students? One may argue that student mental health matters, but what's the point of a mind that can't handle reality? By canceling Murad's speech, the school is teaching its students to prioritize comfort over reality. Does seeking comfort without boundaries sound healthy? Lastly, fighting Islamaphobia is important. But sheltering students is not the way to do it. Students grow from challenges. Challenges are what leads us to rebalance our worldview with more precise boundaries.

Yazidi Nobel Prize Winner Nadia Murad's face juxtaposed with a lioness. Artist: Soloviov Dymtro

Principle Two: Contrast

Contrast reveals key differences

Feeling The Principle: Contrast

Contrast is about seeing differences. In visual arts, such as design, contrast is obvious. Dark is paired against light. Colors are paired against colors opposite on the color wheel, such as blue with orange.

However, obvious contrasts are often predictable and boring in storytelling art, such as film,. The perfect knight rescuing the most virtuous princess from the most evil dark lord is an insult to the modern moviegoer.

People demand nuance. We want subtlety and ambiguity. We want the challenge of deciphering low contrast. Movie characters who give us that force us to think differently. We become obsessed with them.

One such character is the villain, The Joker, from the 2008 film "The Dark Knight." At the beginning of the film, all the protagonists (except Batman's butler, Alfred) underestimate the Joker.

He's just another thug. He's just another crazy psychopath with a shtick. He's nothing we haven't faced before. Their inability to see the Joker's unique threat leads them all to horrendous suffering. They pay the price for failing to see the contrast.

Batman only defeats the Joker after truly understanding what he is: a man obsessed with mocking Batman's sense of justice and morality. The Joker is such a nuanced character that he fills our minds with fascination, inspiring endless debate and new story after story.

In the 2010 animated film "Batman: Under The Red Hood," the Joker captures and brutally murders Robin. Robin is resurrected and swears revenge on both the Joker and Batman. He confronts Batman about his moral code of never killing.

An emotional Robin basically calls Batman a self-righteous prick. How many innocent people have to die because Batman has to prove that he is morally unbreakable? Why can't he just kill the Joker and no one else? Why can't he make an exception? Why can't Batman see the grey area?

Batman replies that Robin is one who failed to see the grey area because he missed an crucial contrast. "*You think the only reason I don't kill is because of morality? It is not just about morality but also my own fragile psychology. Deep down, I am not that much different from the Joker. I am twisted, sadistic, and cruel. If I feed that part of me with murder, I will become addicted, and I will never stop.*"

Artist: Soloviov Dymtro

What Does Contrast Have to Do with Grey Area Thinking?

Grey area thinking is about the journey to becoming more precise. Taking the time and effort to see the nuance leads to that precision.

Nuance is the unique properties of whatever we have our attention on. This is the opposite of seeing generalizations, categorizations, and stereotypes. Those things aren't always bad, but they are often used fallaciously or hurtfully.

Stereotypes feel violating because they de-individualize people. They strip away a person's uniqueness. But, reversely, when we notice the nuances of someone's personality, it can make us very likable because it shows that we took the time to really understand what makes them different.

Competitively, nuance allows us to completely defeat an adversary. When we truly understand the unique position of our opponent, we can create a strategy or an argument that completely removes their reason to fight. Otherwise, they'll just keep coming back for more.

The skill of contrast allows us to see nuance because we can spot subtle but important differences. Grey area thinkers skilled at contrast can successfully navigate complex and ambiguous situations.

Are Subtle Differences Really That Important?

When it comes to problem-solving and strategy, seeing the nuance lets us avoid the trap of fighting the last battle. We have to know the difference between the situation at hand and a similar situation that happened in the past.

Winning chess strategies involve planning multiple moves ahead. These strategies are rehearsed and applied when the opportunity arises.

World Champion, Garry Kasparov, warns his students to clearly see the nuances of each game they are playing. Sometimes, chess players get so excited when they see an opportunity to use a strategy that their mind leaves the current game. They travel to the past, where the strategy worked and led to a victory. But according to Kasparov, a single pawn, one square out of place, can spell disaster for an entire strategy.

The lessons that shape us into who we are can make us dogmatic. We cannot robotically apply what we know to every situation. If we do so, we create avoidable disasters. Instead, we must be present and see the nuances of the situation at hand.

Author's Comments: Limits of Nuance

I had a beta reader who really enjoyed the Batman and Joker example I used to demonstrate contrast. He wrote something in his review that made me chuckle. He used the word "villain" to describe the Joker and then promptly apologized, saying, "I apologise if villain and hero are too black and white, I'm new to this and still learning!"

First, I love the effort. But, if we use my definition of grey area thinking, there are reasonable situations where you can use hard labels such as "good," "bad," "hero," "villain," "right," and "wrong."

Why? Because my definition of grey area thinking calls for us to "respect limits". Human language and expression have limits. We cannot always speak in nuance. Sometimes, we have to use simple language. Writers and speakers have limited time, space, and energy to get a point across. There can be reasonable sacrifices to nuance.

How much nuance we use really depends on the type of conversation we are having. If you and I are at the gas station at night and suddenly, someone charges at us with a bloody battle axe, I'm going say, "Villain! Run!" Fuck nuance (okay...maybe I'd just say "run").

But if you and I were having a highly academic discussion about criminal psychology, then there are probably better words than "villain."

Author's Comments: Differences Between Principles

I got a suggestion from another beta reader to include interactive homework assignments so readers can distinctly tell the difference between each principle. For example, how to sort various topics into the correct principle.

Not important. You can analyze the same topic using multiple principles. The principles all serve the same purpose:

To strive to do the right thing, in the right way, at the right time, in the right amount, for the right reasons, with respect to limits.

Each definition of each principle is just another way of writing that line. The key difference between the principles is the angle you choose to look at something.

All you need to do is determine which angle is most relevant to you. I don't think that hard about it. I just feel it.

Grey Area Structure

"Grey Area Structure" is a section where I use imagery to help Grey Area Thinkers organize their thoughts.

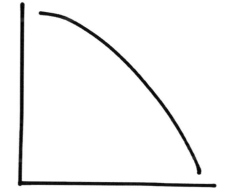

Importance of
Nuance

-Immediate Danger Level
-Casualness
-Big Picture Discussions
-Distance from Main Focus

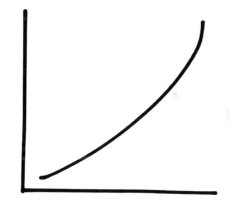

Importance of
Nuance

-Importance of Precision
-Formality
-Detailed Analysis
-Distance to Main Focus
-The G Spot

Contrast. Manipulation and Abuse. Hijacking Causes

Disinformation agents and conspiracy theorists like to hijack the cause of events. They take a real event and distort the cause. A common distortion is to blur the difference between correlation and causation.

Putin's propaganda machine justifies the 2022 Russian invasion of Ukraine with the fact that NATO has many member countries near the Russian border. They say that NATO forces Eastern European countries to join them because NATO wants to attack Russia.

The correlations are true: many NATO countries are in close proximity to Russia. But correlation does not mean causation. No evidence suggests that Poland, Latvia, Lithuania, Estonia, or Finland were coerced into NATO membership.

By contrast, polls show that most citizens from Eastern European NATO countries have a positive outlook on NATO. Take a vacation to Eastern Europe. The average citizen will have plenty of stories of how Russia treated their country in the past.

A far more likely cause is that these Eastern European countries joined NATO because they were simply afraid of Russia.

Conspiracy theorists will take things one step further and use distorted causes to "prove" that their theories came true. For example, they may "predict" that NATO will "force" more countries to join them. When more countries eagerly join NATO at their own free will, they will brag about how their predictions came true.

Contrast. Manipulation and Abuse. False Double Standard

When facing criticism, abusive parties and their sympathizers will do anything to draw attention away from their actions. A common tactic is to accuse others of similar actions and claim "double standards."

A double standard is a <u>principle</u> <u>applied</u> unfairly to <u>different groups</u> for the same or similar <u>actions</u>.

These four factors must be valid for something to be considered a double standard:

1.) Is the <u>principle</u> identical?
2.) Is the <u>application</u> reasonably similar?
3.) Are the <u>actions</u> reasonably similar?
4.) Is the <u>context</u> reasonably similar?

Example: Iranian regime sympathizers claim that Americans have no moral high ground criticizing the brutal death of Mahsa Amini at the hands of Iran's morality police because an American police officer illegally killed George Floyd. Doing so is a "double standard."

1.) <u>Principle identical?</u> Yes. Both criticize police brutality death.

2.) Is the <u>application reasonably similar?</u> No. Criticism of the regime also encompasses religious freedom and tyranny.

3.) <u>Are the actions reasonably similar?</u> No. The regime itself covered up Mahsa Amini's death. Floyd's death was thoroughly investigated, and the officer was arrested, tried, and sentenced.

4.) <u>Is context reasonably similar?</u> No. The American government was supportive of public protests and calls for police reform. The Iranian regime brutally kills hundreds of protesters and refuses to reform.

Your Workspace

How Do We Deal with Willfully Ignorant People?

Use contrast to show impactful differences between ignorance and reality. Don't focus on persuading the ignorant person. Instead, focus on winning over audience members who are watching. If there is no audience, it's better not to waste your time and energy.

For example, mental health is a big challenge for many young people today. Unfortunately, some (notoriously, older generations) dismiss these challenges. They may say this generation is weak and can't handle the real world. To them, there's no difference between depression and sadness or anxiety and fear.

Lecturing people in neuroscience and psychology is energy and time-consuming. Besides, being a nerd isn't exactly seen as powerful.

A quicker way to humiliate them is to demand that *they explain* why courageous, tough young people, such as soldiers, combat athletes, and gymnasts, struggle with mental illnesses.

This question makes everyone see the key difference between mental illness and character weakness.

Remember, *willful* ignorance is a power move. The willfully ignorant aren't looking to be educated. They are looking to humiliate you. In contests of power, you weaken yourself by providing long explanations.

Contrast. Manipulation and Abuse. Corrupted Ideals.

Abusive people justify their abuse by corrupting ideals.

Let's consider an ideal like the "ability to take criticism."

Abusive bosses use destructive criticism to keep a worker off-balance. By doing this, they hide their abusive behavior beneath a corrupted ideal. It also unjustly tarnishes the worker's reputation. This stops them from becoming a promotional or political threat.

If the worker expresses frustration, the abusive boss can say, "This worker can't take criticism."

Luckily, the solution is simple: call it out directly. Show the difference between the true ideal and their corrupted version in front of Human Resources.

"They are corrupting the value of taking criticism. There is a difference between constructive criticism and what they are doing. Constructive criticism comes from a place where you genuinely care about helping others improve. What this person is doing is tearing people down. People who do that tend to have ulterior motives. I wonder what they are."

Contrast. Manipulation and Abuse. Twisting Our Words.

An opponent may attempt to put words in your mouth during a verbal conflict. They may invent a weaker version of your argument to attack instead of your actual argument. This is called "straw manning."

Strawmans are pretty straightforward to deal with. Simply call them out. I wouldn't say, "You are straw-manning me." Most people don't know what that means; even if they do, It sounds dorky as hell. Remember, winning the logical battle doesn't mean winning the actual battle. You must pair your logic with social impact.

Instead, use this, *"I'm going to repeat myself. This is what I said: as you can see, there is a big difference between what I said and the words this person is trying to put in my mouth."*

Notice how I address an audience, not my opponent. I want to encourage grey area thinkers to argue with the purpose of convincing an audience, not an opponent. When you argue without an audience, even if you win, you might be wasting your time.

Some people twist our words because they don't care about the truth. They want to win at all costs. Twisting words is a power move.

Other people twist our words because they are psychologically incapable of seeing nuance. Their brain is so black-and-white, it automatically oversimplifies nuance into contradictions. They can't tell the difference. So to them, you are nothing but a hypocrite.

That's why it is important to educate the audience, not your opponent.

Your Workspace

The names of various logical fallacies sound dorky as hell. "Red herring." "False equivocacy." Ugh... We wouldn't be in this mess if logical fallacies have cooler sounding names. How would you call out various logical fallacies without sounding like a dork?

What To Do If We Are in Confusing or Unknown Situations?

I will share what a soldier who went through the infamous US Military Survival Evasion Resistance and Escape training program told me. *"If you are confused, get to a safe place where you can observe what's going on."*

Manipulators, especially scam artists, want to deny you the time and space to think. You must fight to give yourself time and space. Get to a safe position where you can disentangle fact from fiction.

Grey area thinking cannot replace information and pattern recognition. You can't spot contrast if you don't even know what to look for. Therefore, you have to get to a vantage point where you can observe and gather information without interference.

If you have ever joined a pyramid scheme business scam, you may recall that leaders will tell members to give new recruits as little information as possible. Instead, they try to overwhelm the new recruit with excitement and high energy. Sometimes, they don't even give new recruits the name of the business. That information is only revealed after the recruit begins the brainwashing process.

Why? So they don't go online and read all the horror stories. They want the recruits to be in the dark as they lure them into their territory, where they control all the information. They eliminate space and time for the victim to react, then they go for the kill.

To stay safe in confusing or unknown situations, be vigilant about your space and time. Don't put yourself in a situation where you cannot identify or escape a threat.

Your Workspace

Deep Dive: Iranian Regime Psychological Warfare

On November 16th, 2022, Iran erupted into revolution following the death of Mahsa Amini, a 22-year-old Persian-Kurdish woman, at the hands of the Iranian regime's morality police for failing to wear her hijab properly. The Iranian regime brutally cracked down on protesters, imprisoning tens of thousands and killing hundreds.

According to Iranian rights activist and Nobel Peace Prize winner Shirin Ebadi, 80% of the Iranian population desires regime change, and no dictator has ever survived such odds. But refusing to die without a fight, the regime unleashed its psychological warfare machine.

Unfortunately, the western media played right into the regime's propaganda strategies. By publishing articles without nuance and context, western journalists helped the Iranian regime discredit and disparage the efforts of millions of brave Iranians.

By November 14th, the Iranian regime had arrested 15,000 protestors. Activists and world leaders, such as Canadian President Justin Trudeau, raised awareness on social media about how the 15,000 were in danger of execution. However, on November 15th, all major western news outlets, such as BBC, CNN, and NBC, published articles calling it fake news. Nevertheless, there was no official death sentence for the 15,000.

Outraged at the betrayal, Iranians and their allies were in disbelief at how easily western journalists had been swindled.

According to Iran activist, Elica Le Bon, those reporters failed to see the critical difference between the western judicial system and the Iranian regime's judicial system. In western democracies, prisoners are only punished after a fair trial and official sentencing.

This is not the case with the Iran Regime, which often executes suddenly and without trial. With or without sentencing, all 15,000 are in danger of mass execution. Western reporters had arrived at their conclusion because they did not look beyond the fact that there was no official sentencing.

On December 5th, western journalists *again* repeated this mistake. An article by the New York Times declared that Iran has decided to abolish the morality police as a "concession for the protestors." Again, outrage ensued. Iranian activist Nicole Najafi wrote that "abolishing the morality police" is a meaningless distraction because the regime's laws have not changed.

According to Elica Le Bon, the morality police were not disbanded at all. It simply stopped being a street patrol police. Instead, the branch was converted into a special electronic surveillance unit. This was far, far worse because they used facial recognition to identify women who did not wear hijabs to arrest them at their homes.

Millions of highly-trained, brutal security forces still patrol the street to do what the morality police foot patrol used to do. Western journalists were fooled again.

Many Iranian activists have shared the regime's psychological warfare tactics with me. Many tactics take advantage of the western media's tendency to sacrifice accuracy for a headline. For safety, the identities of the activists must remain anonymous.

An Iranian-Californian told me that during several protests, people with a very different agenda from the rest of the protesters would show up and position themselves so that the media cameras were directly on them. They would then tell the reporters very bizarre or inaccurate things.

After a while, it became apparent that these were people working for the regime. In many cases, they are religious zealots who aren't even Iranian.

An Iranian-Canadian told me that the Iranian regime agents would pose as protesters and spread brutally negative but untrue news about the regime. For example, the regime brutally raped and executed a group of female protesters. A few days later, the story is debunked, and the reputation of the revolutionaries suffers.

Iranians in Iran report that the regime tries to create as much distrust and in-fighting as possible amongst the protesters. For example, during the soccer FIFA world cup game between the UK and Iran, the regime launched a full military attack in the city of Javanrud. They timed the attack with a nationwide media blackout.

Afterward, regime agents spread rumors claiming Iranians from other cities did not care about Javanrud. They stayed home to watch the soccer game.

I will not pretend to be competent enough to advise Iranians on countering psychological warfare. Nor will I give away specific strategies the brave and ingenious Persians are using to fight the regime. But I can tell you that they involve the principle of contrast.

It involves patience and prudence. They carefully observe and analyze their environment. Revolutionaries must spot the key differences between faithful allies and regime spies. They cannot afford to rely on assumptions because being wrong involves capture, torture, and death.

Whenever they get the chance, the Persians go on the offense. They hack into communication between regime officials to gather accurate information and insight. They risk life and limb to protest and protest and protest. Relentless energy. Relentless focus. Relentless attack.

I could not, in good conscience, write a book about fighting abuse and manipulation without talking about the brave Persians fighting the worst of the worst and winning. Instrumental to this fight is the ability to see nuance. We can all learn from them—especially our lazy reporters.

Western media blunders their coverage of the Woman-Life-Freedom protests by failing to take into consideration the Iranian regime's manipulative efforts. Artist: Soloviov Dymtro

Principle Three: Emphasis

Emphasis is knowing when to focus on a value and when to stop

Feeling The Principle: Emphasis

In 2016, I practiced the art of Muay Thai (Thai Kickboxing). Our coach was a tough, no-nonsense African-American man in his 50s. Even at his age, he's the type of man who made you think, *he could probably stop a heart with a single kick to the chest.* Blocking his punches was enough to force me to shuffle backward.

My coach was a strict disciplinarian who prioritized safety. He had zero tolerance for fighters who lost self-control during sparring or landed an excessive or cheap shot on their partner.

Whenever it happened, he threatened collective corporal punishment. We were to line up, and every single one of us would get kicked in the leg. When I was there, he never followed through. Instead, he would change his mind at the last second and make us do a torturous round of burpees and squat jumps. Still, you didn't want to test him.

Anyways, there was this other beginner I was often paired up with during sparring. He was slightly more experienced than me. He had this extremely irritating habit: every time I landed a shot on him, he'd stop the fight, remove his mouthguard, fake-congratulate me, and then give me advice.

At first, I was polite. I told him that words could wait until after the fight. But he kept doing it. He was essentially mansplaining another male fighter to stall his ass from getting kicked. So one day, I landed a good shot. Then, I wait for him to take out the mouthpiece. As soon as he did, I blasted him in the face.

I looked to my left. Oh… I'm fucked. My coach is staring right at me. I mentally prepare myself for what's coming next.

To my surprise, my coach gives me a nod of approval and a thumbs up. Then, he turns and walks away. My sparring partner never repeated his behavior.

Emphasis is about knowing what's important and when it stops being important. It's about recognizing that rules have exceptions.

Nothing was more important to my coach than safety. But he was also wise enough to discern the moment where safety could be reasonably put aside to teach a lesson about ego.

Battle of Sphacteria. 425 BC. Elite Spartans surrender to Athenian archers and slingers. These Spartans were forced to break their uncompromising no-surrender law because Sparta could not afford their deaths. Artist: Soloviov Dymtro

What Does Overemphasis Have to Do with Grey Area Thinking?

In visual art, such as photography or painting, pictures have a focus, such as a model's face. That being said, other things matter in that picture besides the face. For example, the body and the background give context to the face. If the artist excessively zooms in on the face, the meaning of the face is lost because the context is crowded out.

A common fallacious black-and-white belief is, "as long as I am focused on what's important, I can do no wrong."

However, every value, regardless of its importance, has limits. Beyond those limits, it stops being important. Beyond those limits, the value loses relevance and meaning.

Emphasis is about relevance. There's a right time and place for everything. We have to know when to start and when to stop. Going too far with the right thing makes it no longer right.

Grey area thinkers skilled in emphasis know when to follow the rules and when to break them. They read the room and know the context. Because they can see the bigger picture, they understand the limits of their wisdom and expertise.

Author's Comments: Dogma

While visiting a foreign country, I once rented an Airbnb where I witnessed domestic violence. My Airbnb host, who lived with me, would get physical with his girlfriend during arguments, and she would scream at the top of her lungs in the middle of the night.

I discreetly reported the incidents to Airbnb and asked about my relocation options. The next day, I received a text from my host demanding to know why Airbnb had just sent him an email asking him to confirm whether there was violence in the house.

Furious, I called Airbnb demanding to know why they sent that email while I was still living there. A manager replied that it was company policy and told me to call the police if there were any issues. This was a country where police took hours to arrive and often didn't care about such things.

To be fair, the Airbnb staff genuinely cared to help, but their black-and-white approach to policy turned an uncomfortable situation into a dangerous situation. Furthermore, they clung to the fact that everything would be okay as soon as I called the cops. I kept telling them that was not helpful, but they continued insisting.

Had my host attacked me, I would have sued Airbnb and likely won—a costly consequence for failing to see the grey area.

Not every value applies equally to every situation. Read the room. Understand the context. Don't be dogmatic. Failure to do so is toxic black-and-white thinking.

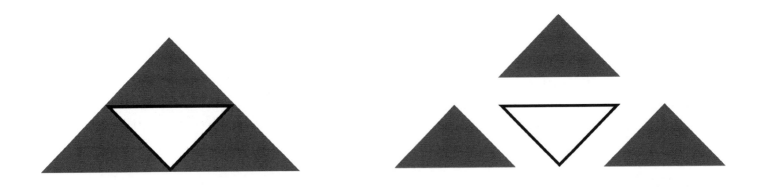

The center triangle's upside-down orientation stops being important once the other triangles are removed. Before, the upside-down triangle had purpose. Afterward, it is just a highly unstable shape.

Likewise, in real life, stripping away context can change a subject's importance. This applies to both information and wisdom. How relevant a value is depends on its supporting values. Take away supporting values and relevance changes.

So Basically, Is Too Much of a Good Thing a Bad Thing?

Yes, this happens a lot in self-improvement. In the late 2010s, positive thinking was all the rage. People were encouraged never to think or say anything negative. In theory, this sounded great! After all, positive thinking is important.

In practice, people started avoiding all discomforts and brushing difficult subjects under the rug. This ruined people's mental health because they weren't allowed to feel negativity. They weren't allowed to acknowledge real emotions, much less confront real problems.

In yoga and hippy communities, "spiritual bypassing," which means using spiritual ideas to avoid confronting real issues, was the toxic norm. As a result, you don't have to look far within yoga communities to find victims of sexual and emotional abuse where the incident happened within the community.

There are plenty of stories where male yoga teachers sexually assault their students and then silence them by saying, "In this community, we only say positive things about each other."

So yes, too much of a good thing is a bad thing. A good thing used in the wrong way is a bad thing.

Author's Comments: Hippies

To see what a modern hippy looks like, Google images of hippy festivals such as "Burning Man" or "Lightning in a Bottle." I won't post photos of hippy individuals because I am trash-talking the entire group. There are good hippies out there. Random individuals shouldn't have to represent all the bad.

"Hippy" is a generic label for someone who abandons mainstream living to pursue non-religious spiritual growth. Their favorite activities include yoga, folk music, and eastern spiritual philosophy. They care about making the world a better place.

While well-intentioned, the hippy community is notorious for sexual assault, narcissistic abuse, and being all-talk-no-action.

Even Grey Area Thinking?

Yes, even grey area thinking.

There is no need to correct someone who says, "Everybody loves ice cream!" Yes, that's a fallacious black-and-white statement. But, ideological consistency is not *that* important.

Grey area thinkers need to be able to read the room and understand the emotional context. Human language has limits. We can't always communicate what we feel using precise language.

Yes, precision is one of the most important values of grey area thinking. However, the precision must be relevant. It's not a big deal to let some things slide.

Is Being Too Restrictive Also a Bad Thing?

Some pleasures come with major consequences. They include unhealthy foods, drugs, alcohol, video games, sex, porn, etc. Many people ruin their health with these things. However, many more people enjoy these things, and it doesn't become a problem.

Therefore, it is abusively black-and-white for society to restrict these things (either by law or stigma) in a way that punishes people who never had a problem.

For example, how many millions of innocent people have been incarnated or executed for relatively harmless substances, such as marijuana, MDMA, and psychedelics?

Over time, extreme restrictions distort reality. Today, in many places around the world (especially Asia), relatively harmless substances, such as marijuana, are spoken about by older generations with disproportionate fear and disgust.

The fear, however, is not caused by the actual effects of the plant. The fear is caused by the extreme legal penalties and social stigma surrounding it.

Is There Ever a Time Where Extremism and Manipulation Are Acceptable?

I said that too much restriction was a bad thing. That also applies to the targets of my book: extremism and manipulation. I don't believe abuse is ever acceptable (well, I suppose there's consensual roleplaying abuse... never mind...wrong grey book).

War is an extreme. But if your country is being invaded, then you may have to participate in that extreme.

If you want to be the best at something, you need to have an extreme work ethic. It may come at the cost of balance, but you must determine if that cost is right for you.

Smiling is the most common form of manipulation. It's also part of being a normal human being.

Allied spy agencies manipulated Axis leadership into making huge battlefield mistakes during World War II—I'm sure as hell glad they did.

There are grey areas where extremism and manipulation are acceptable. However, you have to pay attention to the consequences.

Your Workspace

Where will you draw the line?

Sometimes, If You're Not Going Too Far, You're Not Doing Enough. Isn't Going Too Far Justified to Get Stuff Done?

Your Workspace

Maybe. But that should be a last, last resort. Going too far should never become the norm. So much pain in the world is caused by humans going too far. This is especially true regarding shame and women's sexuality.

Before the advent of birth control, most civilizations needed a way to control the population. Shaming sex was practical. Otherwise, there'd be legions of little bastards running around. There were no DNA tests to prove who the father was, so women took on the brunt of that shame.

However, some people took controlling sex so seriously that they forgot about its original purpose. Instead, they just restricted women for the sake of restricting women.

Abu Musab al-Zarqawi, a leader of ISIS, was a drug-dealing pimp when he was young. Al-Zarqawi's found God in a way many misogynistic womanizers do. Excessive pleasure made him feel so empty that he turned to spirituality.

Instead of doing so quietly and humbly, Al-Zarqawi expected the world to conform to his search for meaning. He did not reflect upon the pain he caused, pimping out women. Instead, he blamed them for his past, scapegoating feminine desire as the root of all evil.

Al-Zarqawi's and ISIS committed unspeakable sex crimes against the Yazidi women of Northern Iraq. They felt neither shame nor guilt. To them, women who do not meet their moral standards are subhuman.

69

Emphasis. Manipulation and Abuse. Controlling Rhetoric.

Many psychologically abusive people control their victims with toxic black-and-white rhetoric. A lover can say, "Who would you be without me?" An exploitive boss can give employees unrealistic demands and say, "Why should I pay you if you don't do your job?"

In martial arts, a fighter who overreaches leaves themselves open for a devastating counterattack.

Exploit the fact that manipulators often take things too far. One effective way to drive home the point is to give them a dose of their own medicine. Use their own tactic against them.

"Who would you be without me?"
"What? Is that what your mother says to you?"

"Why should I pay you if you don't do your job?"
"It won't be your job to pay me if you get the company sued."

Other examples:

"You BELONG to me. I own you."
"So you're saying I belong to no one."

"Only I have the truth. If you don't listen to me, then you are just not ready for uncomfortable truths."
"I'll be ready when you're comfortable with not having the truth."

How Do We Come Up with Good Comebacks?

A good, witty comeback turns the tables of the conflict. It demoralizes and stuns your opponent and gives you control of the fight.

Good comebacks are created by winning the frame game. A frame is how someone chooses to see a situation. A frame game is a battle between two people with different frames. You often see politicians duel each other by playing frame games.

An honest frame follows the law of emphasis. It has a reasonable focus, but it does not overreach. A dishonest frame violates the law of emphasis. There is either an unreasonable focus, an overreach, or both.

When someone uses a dishonest frame, you can counterattack two things: the bad focus or the overreach. For example, let's use a typical abusive lover frame.

"Who would you *be* without <u>me</u>?"

The unreasonable focus is "me." So you can counter-frame by using their own focus against them: *"Is that what your mother tells you?"*

The overreach is "be." So you can counter-frame by focusing on what you want to be: *Free.*

Wit isn't a talent everybody has. Personally, I can do this in writing, but in person, I can't think that fast, so I just grunt and walk away.

Your Workspace

What other strategies can you use to come up with witty comebacks?

Grey Area Structure

Bad Focus		Counter Attack
Irrelevant		Use their subject to attack them.
Distracting		
Misleading		Take what they give you and give it back.
Narcissistic		

Overreach		Counter Attack
Going Too Far		Play along. Help them overextend.
Irrational		
Out of Context		When it's too late for them to go back, reveal their error.
Controlling		

Your Workspace

Deep Dive: Unhealthy Obsession With "-isms"

In today's polarized political climate, overzealous people attach themselves to 'isms'. They often create unnecessary conflicts with other "isms." Liberalism vs. Conservatism. Capitalism vs. socialism. Individualism vs. collectivism.

People are expected to exclusively pick a side. But then, they only see the strengths of their 'ism' and are willfully blind to its faults. As for the opposite 'ism,' only the faults are acknowledged, and any strength is erased.

For example, western far-left intellectuals heavily criticize individualism—the western value promotes the freedom of individuals over collective control. They argue that individualism leads to selfishness and destructive ambitions.

They compare Americans who refused to wear masks during the COVID-19 pandemic to citizens of Asian countries who had no problem with it. Therefore, the west should fully embrace eastern collectivism, which prioritizes the group over the individual.

I am Asian. I grew up in a collectivist household. I also lived in collectivist Turkey for half a year. Let me give you a tour.

In collectivist cultures, your family may decide your career and sometimes your marriage.

Less independence means more neediness and control. Neediness and control mean boundaries offend.

Boundaries offending means the rich and the poor don't mix. Therefore, social mobility depends on looking rich—hence, a more shallow and materialistic society (who buys more luxury goods? White people, or the Chinese and Turkish?).

Innovation and social progress are slow because nonconformity is frowned upon. Until the last decade, racism was completely normal in most collective cultures until western social media told them it was wrong.

Collectivist cultures are hierarchical and usually patriarchal. The father is worshipped, even if abusive. Abuse is normalized and persists through generations because no one questions tradition.

(Yes, I know I'm oversimplifying things, but I'm trying to point out a larger social phenomenon.)

Both individualism and collectivism have positives and negatives. The solution is not choosing one over the other. That is a false dichotomy, a toxic form of either-or thinking. Instead, the solution is to take strengths from both 'isms' while recognizing their weaknesses.

Principle Four: Scale

Scale is understanding that volumes and proportions matter

If you get nothing else out of this book, take this away with you.

Feeling The Principle: Scale

Picture a chef joining the cooking competition Hell's Kitchen. There, he is judged by the brutal Gordon Ramsay, a master chef who screams curse words at poor performers. Imagine that one night, the poor participant forgets to write down the numbers on the recipe he is supposed to cook.

In all arts, especially cooking, proportion sizes matter. Each ingredient in a recipe has a specific volume. Without the volume, there is no dish.

Our Hell's Kitchen competitor is probably screwed. But with some common sense, there are things he can do to be less screwed. For example, if the recipe calls for salt, the chef probably isn't going to dump the entire can in there.

The chef likely wouldn't use the same temperature and cooking time for every single ingredient. He would boil the potatoes on low heat for a long time. He would pan-fry the salmon at a high temperature for a short time. Dried herbs burn quickly, so he would wait until the last moment before tossing them into the fire.

The chef would follow some kind of cooking sequence rather than doing everything at once or starting at random. Perhaps, part of the recipe calls for raw fish. However, the chef knows that "raw" is only a half-truth. So, he responsibly soaks the raw fish in white vinegar long enough to kill all the harmful parasites.

And when Chef Ramsey tells him to get the fuck out anyway, our poor guy wouldn't just drive home using the same speed the entire way. He has to follow stop signs and speed limits. He can't just speed zero to a hundred out of his parking space and all the way back home.

Just like the art of cooking, many things in life won't make sense if we ignore the numbers. We also can't ignore qualities that give numbers meaning. Raw fish is soaked in vinegar to kill parasites. The chef can't just go "durrr, fishy, go vinegar" and throw the cooked salmon in there too (maybe that's why he got kicked out...).

People who intentionally exclude important numbers and meaningful qualities are misleading people with half-truths. Half-truths give us a world with a very skewed reality. All the proportions are messed up.

The principle of scale is about getting the proportions right, which means volume matters.

Artist: Soloviov Dymtro

What Does Scale Have to Do with Grey Area Thinking?

Numbers matter. Most things in life exist on a spectrum. Therefore, when discussing the trueness of those things, the discussion must include specific quantities. True or false depends on volume.

For example, you need a certain amount of water to stay alive. If someone only drinks one cup of water a month, you wouldn't ask, "But how did they die of dehydration? They drank water!"

Quality also matters. The numbers only count if they meet certain conditions.

"But how did they die of dehydration? I saw them drink a gallon of seawater every single day!"

Grey area thinking doesn't work without numbers. Grey area thinking is about doing things *in the right amount*.

Grey area thinkers skilled at scale are excellent with measurements and appropriations.

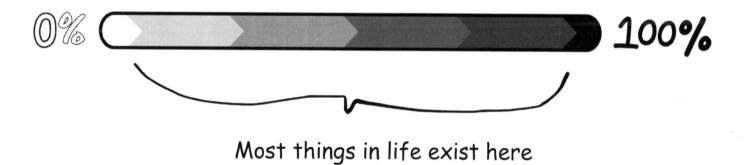

Most things in life exist here

Why Do Proportions Matter?

Proportion allows for relativity. Proportions relate a part to a whole.

From one perspective, proportions allow for scaling, which means building bigger things with precision.

For example, architects draw blueprints of the building they want to build, and the builders will have to follow the final blueprint's exact proportions. Also, the building's bricks need to be mass-produced with exact proportions. This is scaling.

Scaling also applies to the truth. If we tell a story but leave out essential details, we've got the proportions wrong. If our story spreads and influences people, then we would have scaled something that was untrue.

In the second perspective, proportions allow for comparisons. This lets us zoom out to see the bigger picture.

For example, let's say the best engineer in the world gets hired at a company with a formal dress code. The engineer goes to work in pajamas. Nobody says anything because that company needs that engineer more than the engineer needs that company.

However, let's say a random intern sees that and also decides to come to work in pajamas. He is asked to leave. We can say that the intern *lost a sense of proportion*. He failed to see his value to the company relative to that of the engineer's.

How do Black-and-White Thinkers Commonly Violate the Principle of Scale?

By all-or-nothing thinking. The truth is either 100% or 0%.

At the beginning of the Ukraine war, there was a viral news story about a Russian Battlecruiser, The Moskova, calling for Ukrainian soldiers on Snake Island, a tiny outpost located in the Black Sea, to surrender. The Ukrainians stoically radioed back, "Russian warship, go fuck yourself."

News outlets mistakenly reported that the warship bombarded the island, killing all the heroic defenders. Later, this was revealed to be a mistake. The defenders had actually been taken captive.

Russian propagandists and western conspiracy theorists had a field day. Apparently, this was proof that the western media was too corrupt to be trusted at all. The media must be controlled by powerful people from the shadows who want to manipulate us into supporting Ukraine.

How do you take such a minor mistake, which happens all the time, especially during the chaos and confusion of war, and arrive at such an extreme conclusion?

It's called all-or-nothing thinking. In this form of black-and-white thinking, there is no difference between a 1% error and a 100% error. If we only see 0s and 100s, we cannot see relativity. If we cannot see relativity, we lose our sense of proportion.

Scale. Manipulation and Abuse. Volume Suppression.

"Volume suppression" is a term I invented to describe a common manipulation used by abusers to downplay the severity of their abuse.

They take their more severe actions and compare them as equal to less severe actions. By doing so, they gaslight the audience into forgetting that differences of severity exist.

For example, a man who beats his wife every day is finally confronted by an angry mob of neighbors. However, the night before, his wife finally hits back and blackens his eye. So the man's friends go to the mob and say, "Look at his eye! His wife is also abusive. Things aren't so black and white. It's complicated. It's best not to get involved. There's no clear right or wrong here. Let them sort it out."

Volume suppression is also used by regime propaganda. Regimes will use less severe abuses by free democracies as an excuse to justify far more horrendous crimes.

To fight volume suppression, simply call it out. I found that wife-beating analogy very effective.

Author's Space

If someone wrongly accuses you of black-and-white thinking, use the principle of scale to defend yourself! Chances are, they are messing up the volume.

If you are genuinely applying the principle of scale, you aren't using black-and-white thinking.

What Is a Half-Truth, and How Is It Used to Manipulate?

A half-truth is a truth that is missing information. It is a truth told in an untruthful way. It ignores context. It separates the part from the whole. It is merely a part that manipulators pretend is the whole.

Parts cannot be scaled to represent the whole. If you order a burger at a restaurant, would you be a happy customer if you received four pieces of bun and nothing else? Why not? Four pieces of bun have the same dimensions as a burger. How could it not be a burger?

Half-truths are commonly used by propagandists and disinformation agents to distort reality, indoctrinate, or slander. A common tactic used by Russian propaganda is to exploit the truth.

For example, Putin's regime justifies his invasion of Ukraine by saying there are Nazis in Ukraine. Truthfully, there are. What they don't tell you is that the percentage of Ukrainians that are Nazis is no bigger than any other European country, including Russia.

Half-truths can also be used by dishonest marketers, especially in the self-help industry. Self-help entrepreneurs may take complex theories of science or psychology and strip away essential components to build a marketable program. They may even cite research to back up their claims but conveniently leave out key information.

In the long run, following a health program built on half-truths can have unforeseen consequences.

So If Someone Doesn't Tell The Full Truth, Are They Being Manipulative?

Not always. Let's take a closer look. "Reductionist" means being overly simplistic. It means taking something complex and stripping away variables so you can focus on your "favorite" variables.

This isn't always a bad thing, especially in education. In order to teach something complex, we have to simplify it. For example, my deep dive into collectivism in the "Emphasis" chapter was reductionist. However, I acknowledge that I am, and I'm doing so demonstratively.

Reductionism becomes dishonest when it is:
1.)   Falsely implied that there are no other factors or alternatives
2.)   Used to reduce people in a hurtful way

Toxic reductionism violates the scale principle because it tries to be the full truth when it lacks the right dimensions. The proportions are off. Therefore, it does not represent the truth.

Demonstrative reductionism is the exception because it doesn't pretend to be the whole truth.

Grey Area Structure

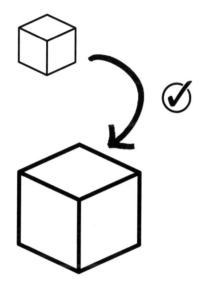

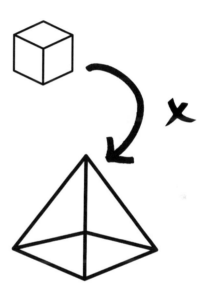

Scale. Manipulation and Abuse. Spiritual Gaslighting.

It is common to hear women who have dated abusive hippy men say that their boyfriends told them they were "manifesting" the abuse. "Manifestation" is the belief that thoughts create reality through psychic energy.

The abuser argues everything that happens, in reality, is caused by manifestation. Therefore, if the victim can train themselves to think only positive thoughts, then the abuse will stop. By saying this, the abuser reduces the victim's world to manifestation and escapes responsibility.

See spiritual bypassers for what they are. Nothing. Neither holy nor wise. Their "wisdom" is but a half-truth of true spirituality. Does the Dalai Lama or the Pope make people feel like shit and then tell them to be positive?

Once you see that, you will break free from the illusion of sainthood they created to control you.

Your Workspace

What are some other tactics bullies use to "reduce" their target?

Scale. Manipulation and Abuse. Projection.

Abusive people may project their worst flaws upon others, especially their victims. They try to accuse other people of their flaws before others can criticize them for those flaws.

Abusers with narcissistic personality disorder use this tactic. It's popular with extremists on both the far-right and the far-left, as well as Putin's propaganda machine.

Narcissists frequently complain that other people are narcissists. The far left will call people fragile from their safe spaces.

Far-right influencers will tell their followers that the left is trying to use fear to scare them into obedience as they themselves are using fear to scare their followers into obedience.

Putin's propagandist Vladimir Solovyov had the audacity to claim that the United States is more autocratic than Russia.

The solution is to attack with sarcasm and satire because these two things give people a sense of proportion. People who project exaggerate. They overreach. Satire lets you out-exaggerate them. When people laugh at the ridiculousness of your exaggerations, they laugh at your target.

"Oh yes. I'm the narcissist. She's a narcissist. He's a narcissist. Everyone is a narcissist but you. Everyone has [list the abuser's offenses] except you."

Author's Comments: Flawed Author

I am not above projection. As I was writing this book, there were moments when I was passionately breaking down a manipulation or abuse tactic, and I stopped and realized, "Oh shit! That's me!"

Deep Dive: Fighting True Lies

Volume suppression, half-truths, and reductive attacks are all forms of true lies. True lies are forms of reality distortion. It is very difficult to play defense against reality distortion because it takes a lot more energy to debunk a lie than to tell a lie.

Deceitful people can simply shotgun an endless volume of lies. This forces honest people to exhaust themselves in fact-checking. Eventually, the defenders of truth will be overcome by attrition. I'm not saying that fact-checking is unnecessary. I'm saying that by itself, it is not enough. Defense is a losing game.

Therefore, we must go on the offense and force deceitful people into defense. They will be forced to turn down the volume of their attacks. Their supporters will expect them to respond. After all, they started the conflict. One way to do this is to strike at the weakest pillar that forms their worldview. For people who use true lies, their inability to understand proportion is their weakness.

Therefore, we can create colorful analogies that demonstrate this flaw. For example, let's say a political extremist is misleading people by using information out of context. They openly mock fact-checkers, demonstrating willful ignorance.

Using a creative analogy, we can effectively attack the foundation of their worldview: *"Information that is missing context is separating the part from the whole. This person is trying to take the wheel off a car and drive the wheel to the store."*

True lies form the foundation of regime propaganda strategy. Russian trolls are paid to spread false narratives that Ukraine is a failed state with a fake democracy. For example, they may label Ukrainian President Volodymyr Zelensky as a dictator because he banned pro-Russian political parties in Ukraine. Yes, he did ban them. However, for perspective, it's standard practice for most countries, including the US, to ban political entities of enemy combatants on home soil. Unfortunately, most people don't know that.

Russian agents take advantage of this knowledge gap. They disguise themselves as Americans on social media to post thousands of true-lie comments in order to sway the American public against supporting military aid for Ukraine.

The most effective strategy I discovered when dealing with Russian trolls is to tell them that I will donate money to the Ukrainian military every time I see them comment. First, I debunk the misinformation. Then, I follow up by saying, "I pledge $5 to the Ukrainian army every time I see you comment. Thank you for supporting a quick Ukrainian victory against the illegal Russian invasion."

Then, I sit back and watch them self-destruct. It's especially hilarious when they've made a fake account pretending to be an American, and they mess up their act. For example, they pretend to be a pro-Trump far-right American and then say something only a liberal would say. And now everyone clearly knows they're a troll. When it comes to fighting deception, a creative offense is the key to victory.

Deep Dive II: Overreacting

I was lucky enough to start college in 2010 before extremism became the norm. Upon reflection, I believe one of the biggest values society has lost in the 2010s is proportionality.

Back in 2010, we knew how to let shit slide. People still got offended, but the punishment fit the crime. If someone said something offensive, we escalated appropriately. A minor comment was met with a minor display of annoyance. A major incident led to a few days of intense criticism. Then, apologies were made, and life moved on.

For most incidents, a dirty look followed by a "bro, that's fucked up" was enough. People who overreacted were considered losers. Long rants about why something was offensive were considered weak, even amongst liberal intellectuals.

Was that world perfect or even ideal? Hell no. There were a lot of problems that needed to be fixed.

But at least in that world, Donald Trump would not have been elected president. Without the left overreacting, there would have been no drama to fuel his popularity. And without drama? Conservatives may not have been seduced.

In that world, social liberalism reigned, with few serious challenges, as the most dominant western culture. Even people who voted conservative pretended to be liberal. Back then, liberalism was cool because liberals were cool.

Then, throughout the 2010s, as extremism on both sides became the norm, proportionality became lost. Minor disagreements now triggered the same level of outrage society used to reserve for murderers and rapists.

First, disproportionate consequences are abusive. You don't scream bloody murder at someone for accidentally saying something mildly inappropriate or being misinformed.

Second, disproportion creates resentment. Extremists take advantage of resentment. At the time of this writing, BBC released a shocking report that over a third of British schoolboys now have a positive opinion of a far-right misogynistic influencer who is currently in jail for suspected human trafficking.

Western liberals have grown far too comfortable with the fact that young generations are predominantly liberal. By overestimating their appeal to youth, the left lost its sense of proportion.

Young people today have fewer visceral reasons to be liberal. They experience far less racism. Their parents don't beat them for sex and weed. They don't remember cool liberals rebelling against that. All they see is liberals overreacting to everything. Screaming at everyone. Forcing their values on everybody. So if you are thirteen years old today, and you want to be cool and rebel against something lame, what is the obvious target?

Principle Five: Variety

Variety is asking "is there another...?"

Feeling The Principle: Variety

When it comes to consuming art, we demand variety. We expect museums to feature numerous exhibitions. We expect streaming services to host a multitude of movies and shows. And when we watch p...never mind.

However, when it comes to thinking, many people get stuck. Not only do they get stuck, they willingly stay stuck. They get upset when others try to help them get unstuck. They insist, "the only reason is this or that." When other people suggest other reasons, they get defensive and double down.

One of the biggest problems this mindset causes is misogyny. Many men worldwide believe they must hate what they cannot get. This mentality is why online misogynistic communities and influencers are so popular amongst lonely young men. Some men become radicalized to the point of misogynistic terrorism and mass murder.

While most men don't go that far, these groups encourage many toxic closed-minded beliefs. For example, all women are a certain way, and men must be manipulative, arrogant, and cruel to be attractive to women. While it is difficult to deny that some women pursue controlling and harmful men, it certainly does not represent all or even most women. In fact, misogynist men may *only* see those women because of their own character and lifestyle choices.

However, misogynistic influencers encourage impressionable men to fixate on a certain type of woman. They want their audience to only see women who take advantage of men. They want their audience to worship the "alpha male" who can supposedly out-manipulate and seduce every woman.

Bitter "nice guys" are especially impressionable because they are willfully blind to women who are happily dating gentlemen. They do not see these couples because seeing them would challenge their beliefs that women don't like them because they are nice.

Throughout history, perhaps the most damaging male mindset regarding women has been the goddess-whore complex: a woman is either a paragon of virtue or she is a whore. Because this standard is so unnatural and destructive to women's mental health, goddess-whore cultures have to resort to more and more extreme restrictions to keep women in line.

If we are incapable of seeing another perspective or another way of doing things, then we will cause needless suffering. Toxic either-or thinking creates destructive feedback loops. Hate what you cannot get, and you will get even less. See only what you hate, and you'll only know what you hate. Force virtue upon others, and they will have even less virtue. (Have you met Catholic school girls?!)

We see only what we want to see. Artist: Soloviov Dymtro

"Is there another choice I can make?"

"Is there another way I can look at things?"

"Is there another solution to this problem?"

"Is there another possible definition?"

"Is there another reason, variable, or factor?"

"Is there another place I can go for what I need?"

"Is there another example that might prove me right or wrong?"

"I feel this is overly pessimistic. Is there another less cynical perspective?"

"I feel this is overly optimistic. Is there another more practical perspective?"

Variety. Manipulation and Abuse. Cults and Isolation.

Abusive people like to isolate their targets. This is especially true when it comes to cults. Cults of all forms (organizational, idea, and personality cults) want to brainwash their victims unchallenged.

Therefore, they cut people off from friends, families, and other sources of information. They reward conformity and punish dissent. They create invisible external enemies to spread fear and encourage blind devotion amongst followers.

These methods have a common goal: they want their victims helplessly dependent upon them. To avoid being the victim, the solution is the opposite: create as much independence from them as possible. The principle of variety helps people achieve that independence.

As an example, take an impressionable young man under the influence of cult propaganda. He is intrigued by their talking points, but he is not yet ensnared.

Before he progresses down their extreme rabbit hole, friends and family can challenge him by asking, "Is there another way you can look at these issues?" Making the target think differently may remove him from the indoctrination funnel.

A second example is a victim who is already inside a cult and wants to leave but feels too scared and powerless to do so. However, by desiring to leave, the victim has already taken a huge first step by asking, "Is there another life I can have?"

Next, the victim must fight for independence. Likely, the abuser has control of the victim's needs.

The victim must ask, "How else can I meet these needs?", "What other bullshit did the cult make me believe?" and "What are some things the cult has not thought of that I can use to help me escape?"

Grey Area Structure

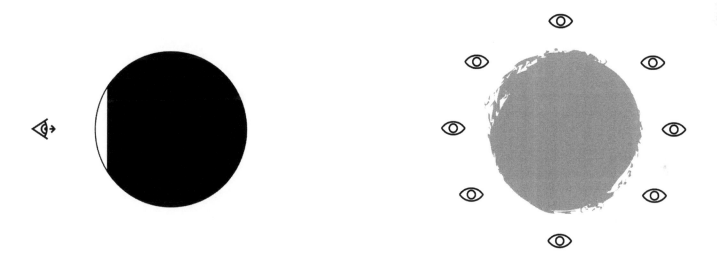

Some people are supremely confident that they have the whole truth because they jump to conclusions after seeing only a small part of the whole subject. By contrast, people who approach the entire subject with a variety of perspectives rarely state that they know the whole truth.

Deep Dive: Is Open Mindedness Overrated?

Grey area thinking isn't the same as open-mindedness. Grey area thinkers can be open-minded, but they are not the same thing. Open-mindedness is overrated because everyone wants others to be open-minded to their ideas.

This includes a lot of bad people. Cult leaders and scam artists hook victims by encouraging them to be open-minded. However, once they get their victims through the door, they work double time to close their minds. First, they isolate them from friends and family. Then, they indoctrinate them to believe that their way is the only way.

Conspiracy cults often boast that they stand for freedom of thought. However, behind the facade is great pressure for their audience to conform. They encourage their audience to "do their own research". But the research must be the same material they provide, and anyone who does not reach the same conclusion is called derogatory names like "sheep".

People who spread misinformation will encourage others to be open-minded to their claims but refuse to be open-minded to the legions of experts and intellectuals disproving them.

Narcissistic abusers, who thrive on dominating others, work very hard to encourage victims to open up to them. As soon as their victims open up, they gather information they can use to control them.

The belief that one must always be open-minded is toxic black-and-white thinking. Not everything that enters our mind is good for us. Some things only mislead us and waste our energy.

Instead of always being open-minded, it is better to be supple-minded. Supple-mindedness is keeping an open mind but closing it *at the right time* and *with respect to our limits*.

Grey area thinkers skilled in the principle of variety have a supple mind. Suppleness is about being versatile and attacking problems from different angles. It's about searching for different perspectives and not getting trapped by one.

If a bar refuses to expel a terrible customer, all the good customers will leave. The bar will be trapped by that one bad customer and eventually go out of business. Likewise, a toxic perspective makes us willfully blind to other perspectives. It demands that we stay open *only* for it. And by doing so, we hurt ourselves.

Therefore, to stay open, we need to know when to close. We don't have to take on the challenge of always being open-minded. Because some people only want us open so they can get inside and close us off to everything else.

Principle Six: Unity

<u>Unity</u> is about deciding what belongs together and what does not

Feeling The Principle: Unity

In the art world, unity is about underlying connections. Artists carefully plan what belongs in their art and what doesn't. For example, both Vincent Van Gogh and Pablo Picasso are famous for their complex paintings created with chaotically meandering lines.

However, as convoluted as their paintings are, they remain pleasant to look at. Van Gogh and Picasso could get away with discombobulated shapes and lines because they followed a strictly limited color scheme. The cohesion of color is what brings unity to their paintings.

The unity provided by their color scheme is what allowed the two artists to break so many other rules of art and still be considered masters.

Unity is about deciding what belongs together and what doesn't. It is easy to see why togetherness is part of the unity principle. But what about apartness? Why is apartness also unity?

In the English language, the word "decision" comes from the Roman Latin words "de-caedere", meaning to cut. Decisions are made by the process of elimination. Available choices are cut down until the right ones remain. Van Gogh and Picasso create unity in their paintings by eliminating all but a few colors.

In real life, connections bring things and people together. We choose our careers and hobbies based on what brings meaning to us. We choose our friends and lovers based on shared interests.

Predictably, separation pushes things apart. We choose to get rid of bad habits because they harm us. We stay away from toxic people because they harm us.

Being able to discern what belongs together and doesn't takes skill and experience. But the efforts will be worth it. Like Van Gogh and Picasso, you'll be able to think outside the box.

You'll be able to quickly identify toxic people. You'll spot and disarm their distractions and their traps. You'll frustrate people trying to scam you. You will be able to make entertaining demonstrations of logic and reason.

Most importantly, you will stop making unnecessary sacrifices because when you understand unity, you look for the best of both worlds. And when you are asked to choose between two evils, you'll look to eliminate them both. And if you can't, you'll build a future where you can.

The licenses for Picasso and Van Gogh paintings were too expensive. So is printing in color. I also felt too bad to ask Soloviov for an Van Gogh imitation after he worked so hard on the Spartan drawing. Artist: Soloviov Dymtro

What Does the Principle of Unity Have to do with Grey Area Thinking?

Unity clarifies. It allows us to resolve ambivalence, which means contradicting ideas and feelings healthily. It harmonizes two seemingly conflicting truths by removing the contradiction.

Unity is the purpose that brings parts together. The parts can then do together what they cannot do separately. Unity can also be the purpose that divides wholes into parts. The parts can then do separately what they cannot do together.

Unity is also the insight to rearrange the parts within a whole. That way, the whole can function better. Sometimes, we may have to add or cut out parts.

Grey area thinkers skilled in unity can see things clearly. With clarity comes reason and the ability to enlighten others.

The Importance of Putting Parts Together.

Sometimes, things are connected in ways that are not obvious. When we see an underlying unity others don't see, we have to connect the dots for them.

The 2015 film "Bridge of Spies" told the story of a cold-war Russian spy captured by the Americans and sentenced to death. In accordance with American law, he was assigned a lawyer. That lawyer, James B. Donovan, worked very hard to save the spy's life and succeeded in winning the court case.

The American public was furious at the lawyer's unusual dedication. They accused him of treason and sent him death threats. But James Donovan stood firm and connected the dots. He asked, "Why should we execute someone for doing the job his country sent him to do? Do we not also use spies?"

(If you want to convince people your argument belongs, ask a question that triggers reflection.)

In 1960, the Russians shot down an American spy plane and captured the pilot. The two countries worked out a spy exchange involving the spy whose life Donovan saved. The American public finally saw Donovan's connection and made him a hero.

When we see underlying unities, we avoid unnecessary sacrifices. Had the Americans executed the Russian spy, the Russians would have executed the American pilot. But, because of Donovan, both men were able to return home.

The Importance of Separating Parts from The Whole.

Ignorance comes from people connecting dots that aren't there.

We combat ignorance by showing the missing dot.

In today's polarized environment, criticizing people from your own political party is rare and unexpected.

Let's say you support a cause, but you have complaints about the way protesters act. A protester is almost guaranteed to say, "By criticizing us, you sound like our opponents. Therefore, you must support our opponents."

The ignorance associates criticism with treason. An effective response separates the association. By doing so, you show the missing dot.

Your reply: "Your opponents drink water. You also drink water. Does that mean you support your opponents? Opponents are supposed to mock your weaknesses. That doesn't mean you don't have weaknesses, and that doesn't mean they only affect your opponents."

(If you want to convince people an argument doesn't belong, repeat their logic back to them using reasonably accurate satire.)

For Someone Who Talks About Unity, The Author is a Huge Jerk to Certain Groups of People. Where is The Unity in That?

Unity does not mean that we are at peace with everybody. Nor does it mean we always try to avoid conflict. Peace based on fear and submission is not a true peace. We don't have to be inclusive to people who don't treat us well.

For example, extremists bullying moderates to toe the line is not unity. That is a false unity. An abusive patriarch who tells his family, "The most important thing is staying together," is not unity. That is a false unity.

False unities are connections created by force and deceit. True unity is built by reason and harmony. Therefore, starting conflicts to fight false unities is entirely justifiable.

Is it possible to create unity by treating our enemies with kindness? Of course! However, that kindness must be a choice, not an obligation. Obligated kindness is not true kindness. The false unity remains.

Your Workspace

117

<u>Grey Area Structure</u>

Unity is about building bridges that connect things others can't see. It's also about pointing out gaps between things that have been falsely connected.

That being said, not everybody is going to want to walk across the bridge you built. Nor will they stop at the gap you exposed. You can't force people to see what they don't want to see.

Your Workspace

The Importance of Rearranging Parts.

Sometimes, a part may belong, but it's not playing the right role. In this situation, we need to adjust the relationship between the part and the whole.

In the self-help industry, many gurus speak about psychology. However, sometimes they say things that sound great but aren't very accurate. For example, "Gratitude and negativity cannot coexist. You cannot be both grateful and angry at the same time."

In actuality, psychologists say that human beings are meant to feel a wide range of emotions. People naturally possess both positive and negative emotions. For example, a person can be angry that they grew up in an abusive household but still be grateful that they didn't grow up in the streets.

Positive emotions, such as gratitude, can prevent negative emotions from dominating your life. However, that doesn't mean positive emotions are supposed to completely erase negative emotions. Psychologists agree that doing so is quite harmful. In fact, it's very common for abusive people to control their victims by guilt-tripping them into being grateful.

Both positive and negative emotions have roles to play. They just need to be put in their right place.

 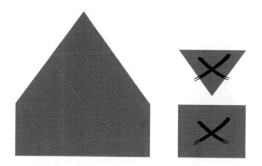

Rearrangement sometimes requires removal. If we hold ourselves to impossible standards of inclusivity and tolerance, then we won't be able to move on to something better. I'm not just talking about social justice. I'm also talking about toxic friends and family.

Unity. Manipulation and Abuse. Entrapping Questions.

Disarm traps by recognizing what doesn't belong.

Let's look at two common traps: loaded questions and forced-choice questions.

Loaded questions are questions that sneak in a false agreement. For example, asking someone who doesn't beat his wife, "Do you still beat your wife?" Regardless if the target answers yes or no, it automatically implies that they have beaten their wife before.

Recognize and disarm: *"I never beat my wife. Why are you trying to trap me with loaded questions?"*

Forced-choice questions only allow you to answer in a way that the questioner wants you to. This is commonly done with a series of yes or no questions.

This is a favorite indoctrination tactic of pyramid schemes. They start by asking recruits, "Do you agree that to be the best, you have to work with the best?" The funnel ends with, "So if you don't join us [the best], then does that mean you have no ambition?"

Recognize and disarm: *"I agree that to be the best, you have to work with the best, but we have very different ideas of what it means to be the best."*

To avoid traps, always give yourself the time and space you need to figure things out. Better for others to get impatient than for you to get swindled.

Unity, Manipulation and Abuse, Fake Olive Branch

The fake olive branch is a trap commonly used by scam artists, unethical debaters, grifters, and cult personalities. The person offering the trap gets the target to agree on a list of reasonable terms. But the trap sneaks in very unreasonable terms.

There are unreasonable terms bundled in with the reasonable terms. If you agree to the list, you agree to the unreasonable terms. And if you sign a contract, you are screwed.

A fake olive branch can sometimes be an entire ideology or individual. Extremist influencers *love* using the fake olive branch. So, how does this plays out? First, the influencer gets impressionable followers to agree on a list of very reasonable truths. Then, they subtly sneak in extreme views and quickly change the subject.

"Hard work is great. Cancel culture has gone too far. Society has to teach morals. Oh, by the way, women should be the property of men. Anyways, back to what I was saying about hard work."

If the line "women should be the property of men" were presented by itself, most listeners will be alarmed and walk away. However, because the message is subtly bundled in with other things they agree with, it is easier to accept.

Author's Comments: Trojan Horse

I believe that fake olive branch traps can seduce inexperienced grey area thinkers if they are not careful. Grey area thinkers are encouraged to see both the good and the bad in people.

The problem is: people know how to gift-wrap their sinister intentions. When we fall for gifts, we ignore the bad until it's too late. Joseph Stalin was as charming and affectionate as Oprah. He could make anyone feel like the most important person in the world. He used that charm to kill 70 million people.

Unity. Manipulation and Abuse. Unreasonable Demands and Conflicts.

To avoid facing justice or losing debates, abusive and manipulative people like to create distractions. Two common types of distractions are:
1.   Unreasonable demands
2.   Unnecessary and irrelevant conflicts

For example, when cult leaders are being investigated for their crimes or lies, they often say something to the effect of, "only those who have accomplished XYZ have the right to criticize me."

Someone who is losing an argument can go for insults or start a new conflict to avoid having to finish the old one.

Cult leaders often encourage members to follow and harass critics in order to demonstrate power. "Stay out of our way. We aren't worth the trouble."

Intellectual bullies elevate the difficulty of their vocabulary instead of elevating their reason. It's a cop-out. "I don't make sense because you don't understand me."

Fortunately, the solution is simply recognize and disarm, just like traps. You can respond to abusive people attacking critics for their accomplishments by saying, "Accomplishments are not the issue. It's your abuse. If you abuse people, it doesn't matter how successful you are; everyone has the right to criticize you."

Your Workspace

How would you respond to the other unreasonable demands and conflicts?

Deep Dive: False Unity

We expect people who are bad at their jobs to be fired. We expect people who are bad at their sport to be cut from the team. We expect men who scare away women to be thrown out of bars.

But when it comes to issues and causes we care about, we suddenly become okay with letting the loudest and lamest voices run the show. So often, not only do we let them run the show, we let them own us. And if we don't do things exactly the way they want, then we become the enemy.

You see this trend in American politics. Moderates on both the left and the right seem to be at the mercy of their radicals. The moderates are forced to tolerate this because "the other side is just so much worse."

To maintain power, extremists use "toxic tribalism." Toxic tribalism is complete conformity to the group. Any dissent or criticism is considered treason. The other side is entirely evil. If you do not fully agree with the group, then you are helping evil. Since extremists lead us against this great evil, they are excused from all bad behavior.

This goes beyond American politics. The Iranian regime violently employs tribalism to keep its population in check. For 43 years, they kept their citizens focused on the evils of western imperialism. Today, Iranians are waking up to the fact that imperialism is not the only evil in the world and certainly not the one they care the most about.

Tribalism may also be present in domestic abuse. In collectivist cultures, abusive families may encourage victims to ignore abuse because outside threats are supposedly far worse. *If we don't stand together, there are enemies who will attack the family as soon as they sense discord!*

False unity is a forced connection based on coercion and fear. True unity is a connection based on mutual respect and shared values. The two are not the same.

This is the reason why, despite warnings from several beta readers, my writing remains abrasive toward people who they believe "need this book the most," aka extremists. One beta reader suggested that I adopt a "teaching tone" because people won't learn if I upset them. Otherwise, these same extremists (the same people who created toxic tribalism to abuse moderates) will simply "tear apart my book" if I offend them.

While I truly respect and appreciate every single one of my beta readers, I must ask: is it right to expect me to teach people not to be abusive? Put it this way, does anyone expect the women of Iran to gently nurture the Ayatollah to abandon his religious laws?

I choose to stand in unity with those suffering from abuse. The people who "need this book the most" can learn from someone else.

Artist: Soloviov Dymtro

Principle Seven: Direction

Direction is considering both long-term costs and benefits

Feeling The Principle: Direction

As a freshman in college, I went home to visit my family after one and a half months of starting school. My cousin and her Harvard MBA boyfriend were visiting my parents. Shortly after I introduced myself, I went on a conspiracy theory rant.

The Illuminati controls the world. The New World Order caused 9/11. You can't trust the government. Rihanna? She's a devil worshipper.

I was meeting Mr. Harvard for the first time. My horrified Asian father desperately tried to save the family's honor by attempting to change the subject. "Show them your six-pack!" (I miss my 18-year-old metabolism)

Nope. On and on, I droned about the deep state, 666 symbolisms, and mass media manipulation.

Mr. Harvard smiled respectfully. He sat patiently and listened in silence. Finally, he cut me a check for $1000, and I shut the hell up. I blew the entire sum on pyramid schemes. Mr. Harvard probably still thinks I am a dumbass. But he never showed it. Not once did his face reveal disdain, contempt, or mockery.

As college went on, I took classes in research methodology, logic, and social science. Afterward, when I rewatched those conspiracy videos, I saw flaws I did not notice before.

My cousin's boyfriend knew what was important: impressing my family. He also had to win me over. I had shaken his hand with a death stare, "Who are you to date my cousin?" Instead of trying to correct me or educate me, he stayed true to his objective. As far as my ignorance, he let time handle it. And time did handle it... painfully.

Direction is about where we are going. My cousin's boyfriend knew his purpose and kept his eyes on the prize. If he had any impulses to correct me, then he stopped to consider the long-term.

By contrast, I didn't know where I was going. At any time, I could have spoken to my professors about those conspiracy videos. Some of them would have gladly analyzed the logical flaws in those videos for me. I was living near a nexus of knowledge, and I didn't even see it.

As for pyramid schemes, I did not pause to consult better businessmen (such as my cousin's Harvard MBA boyfriend) before investing my money and time. If I did, I wouldn't have lost it all.

That's not me! I had a six-pack in college. The other kind of six pack... okay, maybe both kinds of six-packs. Artist: Soloviov Dymtro

What Does the Principle of Direction Have to Do with Grey Area Thinking?

Direction is about pausing to look where you are going. It's about understanding where things will end up. It's about understanding long-term costs and benefits.

Sometimes, massive short-term gains come with heavy long-term costs. Other times, heavy short-term losses may result in massive long-term gains.

Unfortunately, short-term rewards can feel quite exhilarating. Therefore, direction requires wisdom and self-control.

Direction is also about strategy. Sometimes, the obvious next step leads us to a very big and avoidable problem. Sometimes, immediate steps that don't make obvious sense can lead to the greatest rewards.

To do the right thing, we can't get caught up in the short-term or the obvious next step. We have to look further.

Grey area thinkers skilled in direction have vision.

Your Workspace

How Do Grey Area Thinkers Approach Direction?

Grey area thinkers approach direction like a film director. We don't just choose the direction; we must create it. Choosing isn't enough. When we create something real, we can learn from it and adjust.

We can't just sit around all day debating and overthinking the right course of action. At some point, we need something real.

Ultimately, grey area thinking is about constant reflection and adjustments. You can't make adjustments without something real to adjust. In this regard, we can learn a lot from the film-directing process.

First, the film director does a lot of research.

Second, the director decides on the bigger picture: the feel, the tone, and the style of the film. The feel is the audience's emotional experience. The tone is the film's relationship with the audience. And the style is the director's personal expression.

Third, the director breaks things down into workable chunks and executes them. In the process of working with actors, writers, and cameras, the film director can get new ideas and make adjustments.

As you can see, the creative process bounces back and forth from the big picture to the small details. Both inform the other to refine the overall vision. Creating direction isn't always a straight line.

Your Workspace

Grey Area Structure

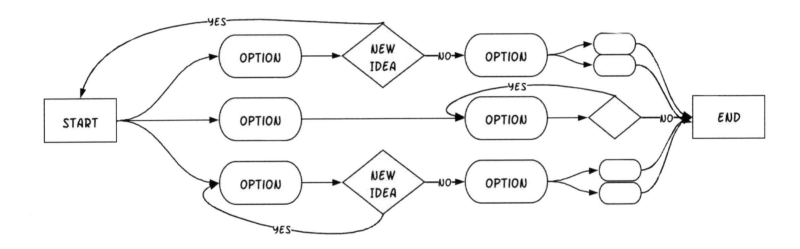

Grey area direction is a lot like the creative process of a film director or a user experience designer. You keep your options open, and you are ready to slide backwards to test out new ideas. The creative process is adaptive and iterative. Just like a grey area thinker's self-reflective journey.

Your Workspace

Author's Comments: Should We Always Sacrifice the Short-Term for the Long-Term?

As an Asian American, I was taught to always sacrifice for the long term. So my answer is FUCK NO. (Editor, let's talk)

Long-term absolutism is hubris. Why? We can't predict the future; we don't know everything and human beings are flawed. With these conditions, always sacrificing for the long term is short-sighted.

Asian children are given immense academic pressure at the cost of playtime and socializing. On the surface, this may appear like a great long-term investment. However, it comes with costs: social intelligence, practical intelligence (street smarts), spatial-contextual awareness (why we are bad drivers) (developed through play), and our fucking childhood. You don't see those costs until you grow up.

Furthermore, not every long-term planner has great values. I know a family who objected to the marriage between their daughter and her handicapped fiancé. The fiancé was a doctor and a good man. The family rationalized their prejudice by saying, "In Asian culture, we consider the long-term. Americans only consider short-term passion." The daughter disowned the family.

Lastly, you only live once, and you don't know when it ends. The 2011 Japanese Tsunami and Fukushima nuclear reactor incident killed over 15,000 people. A young Japanese traveler told me that the tragedy created a massive shift in the mindset of Japanese youth. Traditionally, the Japanese prioritize saving for old age. Today, Japanese youth prioritize having quality life experiences, such as travel.

136

Extremism Is Short-Sighted.

Short-sighted black-and-white thinking creates avoidable new problems every time it solves an existing one.

Consider the two extremes of masculinity. On one extreme, there is toxic masculinity. Toxically masculine men view women as objects for sexual conquest. They have very rigid and harmful interpretations of what it means to be a strong man.

Because they consider emotional vulnerability, compassion, affection, and sometimes intelligence as weaknesses, toxic masculine men often cause a lot of damage to others and themselves.

On the other extreme, there is masculine suppression. In this extreme, everything "traditionally" masculine is discouraged. All men must abandon all traditional measurements of strength, such as ambition, physical prowess, resilience, and pain tolerance. These things are bad!

Ironically, the long-term consequences of both extremes are the same: toxic men gaining massive amounts of power.

Teaching boys to have unhealthy, cruel, and performative standards of strength leads to men being... well, unhealthy, cruel, and fake.

Teaching boys to associate fragility with goodness makes good men fragile (and unattractive to women). It also makes boys who don't wish to be fragile seek out toxic men to teach them how to be strong (and attractive).

137

Direction. Character. Red Flags.

Character determines destination. A person with a strong character but a wrong direction can always course correct. A person with a weak character on the perfect course will fall off. In the long term, bad values are expensive.

Getting too involved with bad characters will also harm us in the long run. Bad characters are good at hiding it, but red flags inevitably emerge.

Therefore, we can't afford to ignore red flags if we are going to enter into a long-term contract with anybody.

Unfortunately, the human mind is complicated. At times, we may find certain red flag behaviors alluring and attractive. It is no secret that abusive people are often highly seductive and are good at getting what they want. Try as we might to avoid them, we often fail and find ourselves either swayed or coerced into their company.

When this happens, it is important not to judge ourselves. Self-hate and self-pity can lead us to believe that we don't deserve better. You are human. Humans have emotions. And emotions don't always obey logic. It's biology.

However, it is still your responsibility to save yourself. You have to seek help and hold yourself accountable. If you are vulnerable to certain toxic character types, then you have to eliminate possibilities where you get involved. Sometimes, that could mean lifestyle sacrifices, so you don't run into them.

Author's Comments:

Yoga wisdom taught me that we often hate the people who have our biggest flaws. And usually, we are blind to those flaws.

As I was writing this book, there were moments when I was passionately breaking down a manipulation or abuse tactic, and I stopped and realized, "Oh shit! That's me!"

Direction. Extremism. Exploiting the Truth

When society is too politically correct, it allows bad actors to exploit the truth. The reason why far-right influencers are so successful today is because they talk about concerns the left refuses to address.

If extremists are the only ones bold enough to talk about taboos, then they control the narrative around those taboos.

For example, let's say a far-right influencer makes an unflattering observation about women or minorities. Even though it's a stereotype, many people agree that the observation has some truth in it.

The standard response by the left is to censor and shame that observation. In the short term, this causes the influencer to receive a lot of hate. In the long run, the influencer can use that hate to manipulate their audience into believing they have been wrongly accused of misogyny or racism.

He can then take the truth and use it to spread other views that are untrue. Maybe that observation was not misogynistic or racist, but other things he said were.

The solution is to take away the taboo. Let people acknowledge the observation and discuss it without judgment. Free discussion will weaken extremist control over the subject narrative.

The observation can then be put into context. For example, maybe a certain group does have certain unflattering qualities. However, it doesn't mean those qualities are an excuse to discriminate or treat people poorly.

Direction. Manipulation and Abuse. Manipulating Back.

By gaining control of the abuser's psychology, we gain control over the abuser. We also gain massive confidence. The following is an interpretation of Frederick Douglass' autobiography by the author Robert Greene.

Frederick Douglass was one of the most famous African-American writers and social reformers of the 1800s. Douglass grew up a slave and was a rebellious one. When Douglass was 16, his rich master got so tired of his attitude that he rented Douglass out to a ruthlessly abusive farmer named Covey.

Covey's frequent beatings completely broke young Douglass' spirit. One day, when Covey approached a very sick Douglass to whip him, Douglass didn't care anymore. In a moment of desperate insanity, he punched Covey in the face.

In the southern states in the 1830s, a black man punching a white man was punishable by death. Covey and Douglass brawled for two hours. Douglass won. A defeated Covey stumbled back into his house. Douglass accepted that his life was over... Covey was probably getting a gun.

But Covey never did. Instead, Covey never laid hands on Douglass again. Douglass understood: *Covey ran a business where he rented rebellious slaves for free and returned them to their masters with their rebellious attitude gone. If word got out he killed a customer's slave, his business was over!*

Douglass wrote that that moment was the turning point of his life. From then on, Douglass would study his masters and get inside their heads. Despite his rebellious spirit, he never got a beating again.

Your Workspace

Direction. Manipulation and Abuse. Mind Games.

More Robert Greene-inspired strategies.

Mind games are usually frequent micro-aggressions or passive-aggressiveness. The manipulator is elusive. If you confront them directly, they may feign ignorance and tell you that you are being too sensitive or petty. After all, the damage is not done by a single mind game. It's done by many small attacks added together.

The strategy to defeat mind gamers is to play it back. They use subtle and elusive tactics to break you over time. So punish them with subtle and elusive consequences. Like an arcade machine, charge them for each game. In the long run, the costs add up.

For example, some people play hot and cold games. One moment, they are highly affectionate. The next, they are rudely withdrawn. They make you wonder what you did wrong. Then, as you also begin to withdraw, they become affectionate again. They use this cycle of unpredictability to keep you off-balance.

Fortunately, when people try to break you slowly over time, they give you many opportunities to learn their tricks. Make time your ally. Observe. Ask yourself the right questions.

Hot and cold. When are they hot? When are they cold? What happens right before they turn cold? What happens right before they turn hot? Do they vary their pattern? If so, what causes them to deviate? How do they make you feel? What are they trying to gain by making you feel this way? What do they value?

Once you figure them out, set your traps. As soon as they go cold, show them you have something they value. As soon as they get hot again, you disappear. Then, come back and say, "Oh, I thought you didn't want it. It's gone. Sowwy." Keep doing that until they are forced to be direct.

Remember, you can walk away. In the long run, do you really want a companion who wants you off-balance? If you enjoy playing the game, then great! However, keep in mind that if you keep winning, that person may go after people important to you who don't like to play.

Your Workspace

Deep Dive: Direction, Helping Others

When we help others, we help ourselves.

Abusive manipulators isolate their victims. This is very common in the corporate world. Destructively ambitious workers may climb the corporate ladder through political games rather than merit. A common tactic is for the climber to befriend everybody except the target, usually a promotion or decision-making rival.

Once the target has been forced out or aside, the climber moves on to the next target. Climbers can rise through the ranks very fast. They hire people just as morally bankrupt and promote them solely for loyalty.

The thing is, climbers rarely go unnoticed. After a few victims, people are generally aware of what's going on. However, they don't want to get involved and risk becoming a target. But as the climber rises, more and more toxic people are brought in and elevated. Finally, the department goes to ruin. Mass layoffs ensue.

I don't expect grey area thinkers to always be the hero. However, people who never help others when there is personal risk are self-saboteurs. In the long run, short-sighted cowardice has a price.

If we don't stand up to bullies, they will gain power. Even if they leave us alone, they might not do so later. The longer we wait, the harder the fight will be when their eyes turn toward us.

For this reason, the United States has a responsibility to protect countries like Ukraine from being unjustly invaded. As the world's most powerful human-rights-based democracy, we cannot allow Ukraine to be conquered by a human-rights-violating regime. If we do, then human-rights-violating regimes all over the world will gain power.

If powerful regime states know that the US will not intervene, they will bully neighbors into submission. Those neighbors could be potential US allies or economic partners. All over the world, new regimes will rise as the credibility of western human rights is lost and the appeal of tyrannical rule grows.

In the short term, all the regimes in the world combined wouldn't dare touch the US or its core allies. But what about fifty years from now? Fifty years of regime states helping each other grow, crush dissent, steal technology, manipulate the world, and undermine the west.

Personally, I don't see the value of living a life without helping others. But for the sake of argument, fuck my bleeding heart. Some Americans only care about America. No one else. American first. However, even with the ruthless attitude that US safety and interests are the only things that matter, protecting foreign nations from being conquered by regimes that hate America *is* putting America first.

Artist: Soloviov Dymtro

Deep Dive: Direction II, Strategic Patience

You may have heard Taoist philosophers preach the wisdom of "doing nothing." What does that mean?

If I could travel back in time to 1933 Germany, would I debate Adolf Hitler? Would I preach grey area thinking to the German public to stop them from supporting Hitler?

It might be too late. I wouldn't just be competing against Hitler and his Nazi party. I would be competing against impossible socio-economic forces that caused the German people to become fanatically loyal to Hitler.

The French poet Victor Hugo once said, "Nothing is more powerful than an idea whose time has come." Unfortunately, that also includes evil ideas. Even if I made Hitler look like a retarded monkey, it wouldn't matter. Enough Germans were already too far gone.

So in that situation, would it be right for me to send German dissidents to their death in pointless protest? Or would it be best for us to work in the shadows? Rescuing Jewish people. Sabotaging the Nazi war effort. Persuading German scientists to defect to the US.

These actions may not sound as badass as making a last stand against the Nazi party, but in the long run, they may save more lives and lead to a quicker Nazi defeat.

You often hear people judging abuse victims by self-righteously asking, "Why didn't they just leave." True, many people absolutely should have left. However, not every abuse victim has the luxury of financial opportunities and a safe passage to freedom.

What if you are a woman in a misogynistic country with no job opportunities? What if you are a young parent who has to stay to protect a child strongly attached to their abusive partner?

Would you go to the police if you were a child of immigrants, causing your entire family to be deported for child abuse? What about somebody with crippling mental or physical illness that would be on the street if they left their abusive support system?

There are plenty of people who made desperate leaps for freedom but missed and landed in more shit.

As fucked up as this sounds, the reality is that sometimes, victims just have to endure. That's just fucking life.

But at the same time, people in this situation cannot accept defeat. They must keep freedom on their mind. They have to work toward that goal. If anything, for their soul and sanity. They have to build toward their desired future in the shadows.

They have to wait for the right opportunities. And recklessness destroys those opportunities.

That's what "doing nothing" means—understanding the direction of where the world is going outside of what you want. "Doing nothing" isn't truly doing nothing. It's strategic patience.

If you don't survive the night, you can't avenge yourself at dawn.

Principle Eight: Performance

Performance is how we do things and what the results are

Feeling The Principle: Performance

Anti-Chinese regime artist Ai Wei Wei once said, "For art to be relevant, it must be political." Political art is confrontational. It awakens the spirit of suppressed dissent. It stands courageously in the face of brutality, demanding justice and radical change.

However, regardless of how good the intentions are, political art is not automatically entitled to applause. That audience includes the people who care about the causes those artists claim to represent.

A common artistic initiative amongst activists today is to stage demonstrations that incite anger in the public. For example, activists may block highways during rush hour. Recently, climate change activists in London threw soup at a priceless Van Gogh painting.

One goal is to get people talking about their issues. Activists also claim a second goal: to teach people a lesson using anger. They hope to make others feel the desperate outrage they feel.

The first goal is easily achieved. People do indeed talk about the causes when they have to sit in traffic for four hours. Okay, but then what? Are those angry people talking about those causes the way the activists intend them to? Or are they becoming bitter opponents and voting conservative out of spite?

As far as the second goal goes, while it is possible to create empathy by pissing someone off, it doesn't work in every situation. There are other factors needed for that to work.

Once upon a time, there was a Chinese emperor who often neglected his duties. One day, his grand advisor walked into the royal garden where the Emperor was playing with his pet bird. Embarrassed, the Emperor hid the bird up his sleeve. The advisor didn't say anything but stayed in the garden long enough for the bird to suffocate and die. Then, he left. The Emperor was enraged and wanted to kill his grand advisor. But he understood the message, calmed himself, and stopped neglecting his duties.

There are key differences between what the Emperor's advisor did and what the activists are doing. First, the Emperor knew he was doing something wrong. The activists' targets do not. Second, the Emperor had a clear call to action he knew he had to take. Again, the activists' targets do not.

What does this all mean? Great ideas and intentions don't matter if the results suck. The principle of performance is about how something is done.

"I gotta go to [work] right now, homie. If I don't get there, I'm gonna get fired... I got six fucking kids to feed... [People] get shot die every day. Deal with it the right fucking way! Not like this." -San Diego resident (2014). Artist: Soloviov Dymtro

What Does the Principle of Performance Have to do with Grey Area Thinking?

Grey area thinking: a mindset that strives to DO the right thing, in the right way, at the right time, in the right amount, for the right reasons, and with respect to our limits.

DO is the end goal. DO the right things. Not *believe* the right things. Not *think* the right thoughts. DO. Grey area thinking is an action-taking mindset. The result of our actions matters, not just our intentions.

Your Workspace

But Don't Intentions Matter?

Imagine if Disney decided to do a crossover between Star Wars and the Avengers. Imagine that the film sucks, and Disney loses a billion dollars. The film's director comes out and says, "My film doesn't suck. The audience is not smart enough to understand my vision. Besides, art matters more than money."

How do you expect the audience to respond? How do you think Disney would respond? (I had a joke involving Mickey Mouse, a dungeon underneath Disneyland, a car battery charger, and the film director's nipples. But I'm chickening out because Disney's copyright rules are not to be fucked with)

Anyway, the example above demonstrates a fallacious black-and-white mindset: "Because I have the right idea or the right cause, everything I do is right. If my actions affect others in a negative way, they owe me their understanding."

Intentions matter. But we have to be accountable for the results and consequences of our actions.

Performance vs. Perfectionism

Grey area thinking: *striving* to do the right thing, in the right way, at the right time, in the right amount, for the right reasons, *with respect to our limits.*

Definition of striving: to make great efforts to obtain something, to struggle or fight vigorously

Definition of "with respect to our limits": we are human.

Grey area thinking is not about perfection. We cannot always wait to tick all the right boxes before we act. Why? Because the right time for action is usually before we know everything.

I want to help protect young people from manipulation and abuse. I wish I had a Ph.D. in psychological warfare before I started writing this book. But that takes about six years. If I wait, that's six years of me not being able to help people.

So I do the best with what I have.

How Can the Principle of Performance Help Fight Extremism?

Action.

Moderate negligence forces people to extremes. The best way to defeat extremism is to prevent it in the first place. Heal wounds before they fester. Do not brush problems under the rug!

But how do we fight extremism that is already here? By building something better.

Outwork them. Outperform them. Outshine them. Not just the extremists on the other side, but also the extremists on your side.

If you see extreme activists do stupid things to raise awareness for a cause you care about, then you must do inspiring things to draw attention away from them.

If they vandalize, you clean. If they block highways, you volunteer to help your local city improve the traffic situation. While they fight for attention by being a controversial jackass, you fight for respect and gratitude by doing the boring hard work they refuse to do.

Start a movement selling delicious food to raise money for the NGOs, researchers, and lawyers doing the real work for your cause. Show the public your dedication, and even if some people do not support your cause, they may respect you enough not to fight against you.

How Do I Get Good at Grey Area Thinking?

If you want to become better at grey area thinking, you need to apply these principles to your daily life. Don't just pull this book out after you get into an argument.

There are reasons why I didn't title this book "How to Fight Abuse" or "How to Win An Argument"

One reason is that if I did that, this book might be obsolete in a few years. Manipulative people will just learn how to use different strategies not covered by this book.

By contrast, the principles of art are timeless. By integrating these principles into your core being, you will be able to instinctively recognize and deconstruct abusive manipulation tactics not covered by this book.

Rather than memorize every tactic I've given you, evolving your natural instincts is far more advantageous.

To become natural at something, you have to live it. Strive to do the right thing, at the right time, in the right amount, for the right reasons, in the right way, and with respect to limits in all that you do.

Make decisions like a grey area thinker. Make plans like a grey area thinker. Make love like...wrong grey book.

Nah... right grey book. Make love like a grey area thinker.

Performance. Manipulation and Abuse. Fighting Back.

To perform well, you must pick the right performance. To fight well, you must pick the right fight.

In warfare, you have to have a clear objective. Armies that fight without clear objectives lose. Preferably, you also have a clear role. Knowing your role saves you time and energy.

The basics of actual warfare also apply to individual conflicts against abusive and manipulative people.

In war, you have to know the terrain of the battle. Where does the fight take place? Is that environment right for your skillset and limitations? In that setting, what is possible and impossible?

How well are rules enforced? For example, if it is a debate, can your opponent interrupt you without penalty? Can they make shit up with impunity? What does the crowd want? Is a logical argument a winning argument? Or do they want entertainment and humiliation?

In war, you have to know yourself and your opponent. Does your opponent have habits that get on your nerves? Are they ignorant? Do they cheat? Do they lack integrity?

If your opponent has character flaws, avoid complaining about them. If they know something bothers you, but you can't stop them, they will use it more. Instead, pick a fight where you can exploit those flaws.

Author's Comments

I once saw a Russian propagandist harassing a Ukrainian blogger online. They were arguing about history. I had no idea about history, but I understood the propagandist's manipulative tactics. So I jumped in and focused my efforts entirely on exposing those tactics.

I ignored the propagandist's attempt to engage me in other ways. Instead, I let the blogger handle the history. Together, we humiliated him and denied him the opportunity to spread misinformation.

We were successful because I knew my objective and stayed within my role. My goal was to help a Ukrainian blogger defeat Russian misinformation. My role was to support her so she could put all her focus into content and not have to worry about traps and tricks.

As soon as we broke our opponent's confidence and ensured he could not influence a neutral audience, we exited and let him babble to himself. Our job was done.

When Should We Avoid Battle?

It is best to avoid battle if:
1. You lack a clear and meaningful objective
2. You can't perform
3. There's no worthwhile reward

Fight when you decide to. Don't let enemies provoke you into a fight. In warfare, an army with a clear objective can overcome a more powerful army with unclear motives.

When enemies provoke you into battle, you lash out without an objective. Meanwhile, your enemy has a clear objective to harass, distract, or entrap you.

Furthermore, you cannot perform at your best because you are emotionally compromised. In fact, your opponent might have tricked you into a conflict where you don't even have the tools to win.

Think about the recent American military defeat in Afghanistan. The United States fought for twenty years without clear and meaningful objectives. Americans won every single battle but ultimately lost the war.

The best fights are high-reward, low-cost. Pick fights that yield the greatest rewards, but cost the least energy.

Do not let your enemies sucker you into endless low-reward, high-cost battles.

Performance. Manipulation and Abuse. Not Fighting

The best defense is to not be attacked.

As the writer of this book, I am going to piss off a lot of people. The far-left. The far-right. Conspiracy theorists. Russian regimes. Iranian regimes. Hippie regimes. They will not be leaving me alone. I can't stay anonymous. I can't play dumb.

But my readers can. So take advantage of being invisible, unreachable, and uninvolved. Emerge at the right time for the right reasons.

Fights drain energy. Victory inspires revenge. Defeat brings humiliation. Mere participation can harm your social prospects.

I taught my readers how to fight. However, just like learning martial arts, you learn to fight so you don't have to. When you have the skill to win a fair fight in your head, you can walk away with confidence without needing to prove yourself.

Besides, people who can't beat you in a fair fight may pull out knives and guns. Extremists and abusive people don't fight fair. Do people who draw weapons in a fistfight listen to demands for a fair fight?

So instead of fighting them, do what Patrick Swayze says, "Be nice, until it's time not to be nice."

Deep Dive: Performance, How I Wrote This Book

Originally, the performance principle was supposed to be rhythm. In art, rhythm is about the pattern the audience follows. It's about the experience it creates.

As a writer, I hear a lot of advice about the "right way to do things." You are supposed to write every single day. You are supposed to cite research and empirical evidence. You have to try not to be biased. Don't use anecdotes. You must be persuasive and nice and avoid telling people they are wrong.

I broke every single one of those rules. If I followed them, I simply couldn't write with my heart. If I don't write with my heart, my writing sucks.

I tried writing every day. My writing sucked. I kept doing it because I wanted to feel disciplined, but it still sucked. Then I took a break, volunteered in Ukraine, came back, wrote, took another break, and wrote some more. My writing sucked less.

After a period of trial and error, I discovered a rhythm that worked for me: a phase of moderate writing (1-3 hours a day), a phase of intense writing (6-12 hours a day), and a break (0 hours a day). That rhythm wrote this book.

In life, we will hear a lot of advice about how we should do things. But to do our best work, we must do what works for us. We can't just assume what works for others works for us.

I did not cite empirical research. I know how. I'm educated. But I'm also not looking for academic accolades. I am trying to give everyday people tools to fight abuse, manipulation, and extremism. And most people don't give a shit if I write, "According to a study done by Smith and Jones (2009)..." They want to know how to stop hurting.

I use anecdotes because stories are powerful. Mass manipulators tell stories. They don't share studies. I understand that anecdotes have flaws, but they bring out my best writing. And I will not deny my readers that.

I do not try to hide my bias because being fake hurts my writing. I do not try to persuade extremists. I am not a negotiator, and I won't pretend to be.

What I do know is teaching people how to fight. I am not encouraging people to be combative, but I want to give people the confidence that they can if they have to. That's my grey area thinking.

Grey area thinking is about doing things with respect to your limits. Limits don't have to be limiting. Limits can encourage us to use what we have to the best of our ability. Sometimes, it is better to master what you own instead of looking for more.

My limits don't fall within the rules. I had a choice to expand my limits or use them. To give my best performance, I chose to use them.

Deep Dive: Losing Battles and Winning Wars

For marketing reasons, some have suggested that I name this book "How To Win An Argument." As I've explained previously, grey area thinking is bigger than that.

But since this topic is so popular, here is the secret to winning every single argument for the rest of your life. First, be the dumbest person in the world. Second, abandon all morals. Third, the truth doesn't matter; only you do. Fourth, have zero empathy. Do those four things, and you will never lose an argument again.

It takes wisdom, decency, and self-control to lose an argument. When wise people debate with each other, they don't argue. They discuss. It's a dance. Not a fight. They yield to allow the other person to make their strongest point. In the end, neither person wins. The truth wins.

In chess, the queen is both the strongest and the weakest piece. The queen's supremacy means that your opponent will sacrifice any weaker piece to kill her. Thus, the queen spends a lot of time hiding.

Likewise, the wise hide from the unwise because the unwise can defeat the wise by doing things the wise refuse to do. But is it wise for us to never argue with the unwise?

Well, the Russian regime certainly counts on it. That's why they pay millions of dollars a year to trolls to argue online. Putin wouldn't bother if those trolls couldn't keep the wise from sitting out.

If the wise never argue against the unwise, then the unwise will simply take advantage of their absence. So sometimes, the queen has to get her hands dirty and get into a mud fight with the pawns. Sometimes, you just have to fight battles you know you can't win, so you can win the war.

If you must fight a battle you can't win, then lose on your terms. Lose spectacularly. Make their victory meaningless and costly.

For example, if you are arguing against an online troll, destroy their reasoning quickly and impactfully. When they start twisting your words and playing mind games, sarcastically admit defeat. Stop being serious and start being playful. You will win the neutral audience, and that's what truly matters.

Strategic defeat is far more meaningful than empty victory—and it costs far less energy. For example, let's say a domineering person keeps interrupting you during a debate. Give up. But before you give up, make the audience want more of you. Make them resent your opponent for taking your performance away from them.

The most common mistake people make when fighting abuse and manipulation is that they work too hard. They throw everything at them. All their intellect. All their heart. At someone who can't even comprehend those things. Just let them win! But in the process of losing that battle, complete objectives that ultimately win the war.

Artist: Ulyana Dikhtyar

The Elements of the Art

The Elements

Besides the universal principles, every art has unique elements. Painting has colors, lines, and shapes. Film has acting, writing, lighting, cinematography, and sound. Martial arts has punching, kicking, grappling, and movement.

The element of thinking art is the thinker itself. They are the grey area thinker's emotions, courage, wisdom, humility, character, social ability, and literacy. Together with the principles, they create art. While this section is the shortest of the book, please do not underestimate its importance.

Grey area thinking is an action-oriented mindset. Thoughts do not take action. Thinkers do. Recall my definition of grey area thinking: striving to *DO* the right thing, in the right way, in the right amount, at the right time, for the right reasons, and with respect to our limits. Principles do nothing without the elements.

Element One: Accept Emotions

The Significance of Emotion

Human beings are emotional creatures before we are rational creatures. It's science. Our brain's limbic system, which governs our emotions, is far more powerful than our cerebral cortex, which governs our logic.

Emotions do not go away simply because we want them to. We can control them. We can suppress them. We can redirect them. But we can't erase them.

Those who act like they can are full of shit. Some people are too proud of their logic. They may claim they "have no emotion" and live life purely based on reason.

If you want to know what people who truly "don't have emotions" are like, you can find documentaries on people with damaged limbic systems. Trust me; it's not something you want.

People who are overly proud of their logic are often the most driven by emotion. They just refuse to be aware of it. But they reek of pride, fear, anger, and contempt.

Their negative emotions lurk beneath their subconscious, manipulating their logic like a puppet on strings. When others point out something irrational they said, they usually respond with anger and demand recognition for how perfectly logical they are.

The Significance of Emotions

Grey area thinking requires clarity. People without emotional intelligence (EQ) will be highly limited. First, they will not be **balanced** individuals. If they refuse to acknowledge their emotions, they won't even know what their true needs are. If they don't have empathy for other people's emotions, then they won't understand the needs and boundaries of others.

Second, they will be terrible at applying the principle of **emphasis**. Low-EQ people tend to hang on to hard rules for dear life. They don't have the flexibility to loosen their grip when the situation calls for bending the rules. They act like computer programs. And when the program encounters an unknown scenario, they freeze up and stop working.

Third, low-EQ people frequently violate the principle of **scale**. They don't understand appropriate volume. They struggle with proportion. They overreact. Their worldview is more likely to be all-or-nothing. These are the extremists who say, "You are either fully with us or fully against us."

They are psychologically incapable of fathoming any other option, which leads them to violate the **variety** principle. They struggle to look at things in a different way. Because to do so requires us to admit that our rationality has limits (**emphasis**).

Emotions and Extremism

According to Sam Katz, author and expert on terrorism, not everyone who joined ISIS was illiterate, contrary to popular belief. A significant proportion were college graduates from moderate middle-class families who couldn't find jobs. Their families were shocked. Their kids weren't monsters—at least, not until the quarter-life crisis.

Even highly-educated people are capable of incredible stupidity when they are emotionally vulnerable. Existential crises are not resolved logically. They are resolved emotionally. When people try to fill emotional wounds with logic, they go down rabbit holes controlled by negative emotions. The correct solution is to become aware of your emotions and feel your way out of the trap.

Using ideology to fill emotional wounds is a gateway to extremism. It's like trying to get nutrients by eating fast food. You just end up eating and eating and eating, but you are not getting what you need. Oh, and now you're addicted to fast food.

Emotions, Abuse, and Manipulation

In the Batman lore, the supervillain, the Joker, seduces his psychiatrist Harley Quinn and abuses her as a lover. Harley is hopelessly addicted, and regardless of how the Joker treats her, she keeps going back to him. Finally, after years of torment, she leaves him for good and becomes an assassin for the US government.

In the 2021 film "The Suicide Squad," Harley Quinn, played by Margot Robbie, is on a CIA mission in a fictional South American country. However, she is captured by the enemy and brought to their dictator, who seduces her. After they make love, the dictator begins talking about his plans for mass murder.

Before he even finishes his sentence, Harley shoots him in the heart. She then apologizes to his dead body. She explains that because she has such bad taste in men, she made a self-promise to immediately kill any lover who raises major red flags.

In a way, Harley demonstrates grey area thinking perfectly. She knows that she has an emotional weakness for certain types of men. So she sets a hard boundary for herself and removes the obstacle immediately—textbook application of the **balance** principle. Harley uses emotional intelligence to understand her psychological limits. She knows if she does not act immediately, she risks falling for the dictator and repeating what she had with the Joker.

Harley understands that because she is attracted to mass murderers, it is reasonable for her to go for the immediate kill. She acts with appropriate proportionality, demonstrating the **scale** principle.

Her long-term vision and self-knowledge demonstrate her grasp of the **direction** and **performance** principles. She does the right thing, at the right time, in the right amount, and with respect to her limits.

Please don't kill your toxic lovers. However, do understand that manipulators go after our emotions. Like Harley, we need to understand and accept our emotional weaknesses rather than pretend we don't have them. If we can control them, great! If we can't, then we need a contingency plan.

Element Two: Courage

The Significance of Courage

Avoiding conflicts is often the wiser option. However, if we do not have the courage to fight, then we can't protect what matters when it needs us the most.

Conflicts can often be healthy. A good conflict can save a worthy friendship that is being slowly driven apart by failure to respect boundaries. A good conflict can stop small problems from festering into big problems.

Conflict can bring us clarity. A good argument can sometimes help us clarify our ideas and beliefs. Clarity can help us create powerful statements that resonate deeply with people.

I believe those who lack courage cannot reach high levels of wisdom or compassion. If we lack courage, we cannot know if we avoided conflict due to wisdom or fear. If we lack courage, we cannot know if we show kindness out of compassion or agreeableness.

Without courage, we won't always know if we are doing the right thing for the right reasons. Without courage, we can only do the right thing if courage is not needed.

The Significance of Courage

Zhuge Liang (181 AD to 234 AD) is regarded in folk stories as one of the greatest military strategists in ancient China. He was defeated by a warlord named Sima Yi (179 AD to 251 AD).

When Zhuge and Sima went to war, Zhuge had a disadvantage: food supply was a constant problem. Sima didn't need to defeat Zhuge on the battlefield. He just had to stall until Zhuge ran out of food and was forced to retreat. Sima avoided battle as much as he could. Zhuge was desperate for a fight, so he started a propaganda campaign branding Sima as a coward.

One day, Zhuge sent a messenger to Sima's camp to insult him. Sima patiently allowed the man to roast him in front of all his generals. When he was finished, Sima politely asked the messenger, "How is your master's health?"

The messenger replied that it was great. Sima then asked, "Does your master sleep well?" The messenger replied that his master was so busy managing every detail of the army that he rarely slept.

Sima bade the messenger (who was probably prepared to die) farewell and had him safely escorted out of the camp. Then, he turned to his generals and smiled, "Zhuge Liang will be dead within a year." Sure enough, Zhuge Liang died from stress and overwork a year later. The Sima family then conquered all of China.

Courage takes on different forms. Sometimes, courage isn't charging into battle to prove yourself. Sometimes, courage is enduring blows to your reputation as you work toward a vision others can't see.

Of all the different ways to express courage, I would argue that maintaining strategic patience while being called a coward requires the most. In some cases, the danger is more than just insults. Followers who demand action will try to remove you from power. And pissed-off dependents are far closer to you than your enemies.

Direction requires courage. Because when you play the long game, you are going to upset a lot of short-sighted dependents, and your opponents will use that against you.

Courage, Abuse, and Manipulation

The most effective manipulators go after our demons. They go after our fears, insecurities, and the parts of ourselves we hate.

Courage let us confront our own demons so that they cannot be used against us.

In life, we will discover things that we wish weren't true. The sooner we confront them, the sooner we can begin to **rebalance** our worldview.

If we don't rebalance, then the ugly truth will always be there to haunt us. If we see examples of that ugly truth, we will run. Eventually, a manipulator can offer us a sweet lie to resolve that ugly truth.

Without courage, manipulators can seize control of our **balance**.

Courage and Extremism

Extremists exploit social taboos. They talk about the things their opponents wish were not true. Then, they use that to spread things that are untrue.

The far-right loves to go after problems the left tries to brush under the rug. One current issue is cancel culture on college campuses going too far. When liberals try to bring these issues up, other liberals may punish them. Professors have been fired for doing so.

Therefore, the far-right controls the taboo's narrative, attracting vulnerable people. They can then say to these vulnerable people, "Cancel culture means that universities are actively brainwashing their students, and information from higher education can no longer be trusted. Here, believe my conspiracy theories instead."

To successfully confront extremism, we must have the courage to look under our rug. We have to clean up the problems we've swept underneath and endure the insults of those who are too cowardly to look.

Element Three: Wisdom to Be Silent

The Significance of Silence

There's an old African proverb, "A speaker of truth has no friends."

If you walk around acting like you know better than everyone, then you run the risk of no one listening to you when you really need them to. Therefore, applying the **balance** principle, we must form boundaries against our need to speak.

Are we giving someone advice because they need to hear it or because we want control? Are we arguing to stand for something, or are we arguing because we want to dominate someone?

With respect to the **contrast** principle, there's a big difference between saying what's right and doing what's right. Speaking isn't always the best course of action, even if we are right.

A good way to know the difference is to apply the **direction** principle and ask ourselves, "What's the long-term cost and benefit of speaking vs. staying silent?" If speaking now makes people less receptive to our words in the future, it is better to stay silent.

If we need to speak, we should apply the **scale** principle and choose the right volume of words **balanced** with the right volume of silence.

The Significance of Silence

We all know people who have to give their unsolicited opinion and advice on every subject. We instinctively feel repulsed.

Why? Because people who are constantly advising aren't observing. They aren't listening. They don't care to understand. They care about their egos.

During the Ukraine War, an American firearms instructor volunteering to train Ukrainian soldiers was accused of causing the death of a Ukrainian soldier wounded at the Battle of Bakhmut. The American volunteer had zealously taken charge of providing medical aid to the wounded soldier. He had no formal medical training. There were trained medics nearby, ready to do the job.

I don't have enough information to accuse this man of risking lives to play the hero. But I will say he acted very unwisely. He refused to respect the limits of his expertise. He grossly violated the **emphasis** principle by refusing to stop when he should have.

Silence and Extremism

Loudness is a common trait shared by extremists from every single group. The far-right screams at everybody that they have the truth. The far-left screams at everybody that they have the truth. Terrorists blow shit up to declare that they have the truth.

You just want to shake these people and say, "Look bitch, the truth doesn't need superfans. It needs people to work for it."

How do you work for the truth? By emptying your cup.

Once upon a time, a Zen master had a student who wouldn't shut the fuck up. Every time the teacher told a story, he told one of his own. Every time the teacher shared insight, he interrupted with his own ideas and beliefs.

So the teacher said, "Let's have tea." He gave the student a cup. He fills it with tea but doesn't stop pouring. He keeps going and going. The student, who is getting burned by the hot tea, is screaming for him to stop.

The teacher then said, "This you, bitch. Full of ideas and can't shut up. Now get the fuck out and come back when you've emptied your cup."

Silent Strategies Against Abuse and Manipulation

Silence lets us observe. Observation yields insight to help us catch subtle cues that reveal a manipulator's intentions.

Silence allows you to survey your environment and analyze potential threats. Silence is a boundary that can protect your wellbeing. It gives you time and space to gather information and make plans.

Silence can stop you from committing to the wrong allies. It lets you pause before you make promises that you will later regret. It stops you from joining in on gossip and saying hurtful things.

Silence stops you from revealing information to people who will later use it against you.

Silence can sometimes stop toxic behaviors from others. You can warn people that you are not happy by creating uncomfortable tension using silence. By doing so, you also demonstrate power by remaining calm and in control.

When using silence to control social outcomes, it's important to respect the **emphasis** principle. Silence at the wrong time leads to confusion or problem avoidance. There's a time for silence and a time for words. Be versatile enough to do both.

Element Four: Self-Reflection

The Significance of Self-Reflection and Ego Management

Grey area thinking is about a lifelong journey of self-reflection and adjustment. If we don't have the ability to be wrong, then grey area thinking isn't for us.

We have to take ownership of our self-reflection because we can't always rely on others to give us feedback. Most people aren't comfortable telling us our flaws. Others may advise us in ways that are controlling or self-serving. Therefore, it's better to take the initiative to explore our inner world.

We must keep the principle of **emphasis** in mind. Too much introspection can be unhealthy, especially if it is done without self-love. The key difference between healthy and loveless self-reflection is self-image. Are we self-reflecting to be better, or are we self-reflecting to be someone else? (**contrast**)

As grey area thinkers, we should strive to fix our own bullshit before calling others out on theirs. If we are too focused on others, then we aren't spending enough time with ourselves. And with respect to the **unity** principle, it takes a lot of work to figure out what belongs in our lives and what doesn't.

Self Reflection, Abuse, and Manipulation

If we do not have the ability to be wrong, then manipulators only need to get us once. If we take ourselves too seriously, we are bound for humiliation. Humility is insurance against humiliation.

In college, I fell for three pyramid schemes. Lost thousands of dollars. Lost hundreds of hours. Each venture ended in disaster. Yet, I kept going back for more. I was fucking idiot.

And that's okay. I learned a lot of hard lessons by being an idiot. But I had to be open to the possibility of being wrong.

There are people a lot smarter than me who stay for years and years with a destructive ideology because they are too proud to admit they got swindled.

Element Five: Character Before Ideology

The Significance of Character

Grey area thinking does not need superfans. Grey area thinking needs people with strong characters to practice the art. Ultimately, grey area thinking is only as powerful as the grey area thinker.

If we want to spread grey area thinking, we should seek to inspire people with our character first. Ideology should come second.

We should treat character like a healthy diet. Like a healthy diet, a healthy character consists of a wide variety of qualities, not just a few favorites. Qualities include integrity, compassion, authenticity, empathy, work ethic, courage, and others.

Without **variety**, we will become one-dimensional, which can be destructive. People who only care about success-bringing qualities, such as ambition, while neglecting soft qualities, such as compassion, should not be surprised when they accumulate opposition. People are right to be concerned with a success that harms society.

Likewise, people who only care about soft qualities, such as tolerance, while neglecting hard qualities, such as toughness, should not be surprised to see eyes roll. It's in our DNA to be turned off by those who act like they'd be completely helpless in the stone age.

The Significance of Character

We can build character without acting like we are better than everybody. It's natural to get upset at people who don't have the qualities we have. A thoughtful person will get extra upset at an inconsiderate person. Hardworking people can't stand lazy people. An authentic person may be disgusted with fake people.

It's important to realize that everybody has their own journeys. People have battles others can't see and puzzles others wouldn't know what to do with. Therefore, we should avoid character contests and judgments as much as possible.

When I feel judgmental, I try to redirect my ego against my own flaws. I try to remember that there are people with qualities I don't have. I imagine how I would feel if they looked down on me for not meeting their standards.

However, it is wise to analyze character when we choose our friends. The wrong friends can lead us in the wrong **direction.**

When we choose friends, we should prioritize character over ideology. Ideals are surface deep. Character is core deep. In the long run, ideals fade, and character stays. Someone with "good" ideals but a bad character may abandon (or corrupt) those ideals. Similarly, someone with a good character but "bad" ideals may also abandon those ideals.

Character and Extremism

An army disciplines its warriors before sending them out to fight. When we have a cause we care about, we can get so fixated on finding like-minded people that we ignore the content of their character.

But we have to remember that words are easy. Action is hard. Ideals do not act. Characters do.

I have seen hippies write poetry about compassion that is so beautiful it would make the Dalai Lama blush with envy. Then, they turn around and abuse their lovers.

You may have noticed that despite the fact that I claim to be liberal, I criticize the far-left far more than I criticize the far-right. I must be a secret sympathizer!

Or perhaps, another reason (**variety**) is that to get people to stop joining the far-right, you have to clean up the mess on your side first. What's the point of me attacking the far-right if people just look at my side and say, "Ew...?"

Element Six: Growth Mindset

The Significance of a Growth Mindset

A growth mindset is the belief that abilities, relationships, and success can be developed with time and effort. By contrast, a fixed mindset is the belief that these things are predetermined and unchangeable.

For example, two people start playing chess. They both suck. One has a fixed mindset, and the other has a growth mindset. The fixed-minded will likely quit sooner. The growth-minded will be less likely to give up, less frustrated by loss, and given time, become highly skilled.

A fixed mindset is not compatible with grey area thinking. By its nature, the fixed mindset is a fallacious either-or fallacy. *Either, I'm good at something, or I'm not. Either something is destiny, or it's not.*

Because grey area thinking requires a lifelong journey of reflection and adjustment, having a growth mindset is essential. The principles and elements of grey area thinking require time and effort to learn.

It took me a lifetime of failure to become a grey area thinker. I intend for my readers to have an easier journey. However, that journey requires a growth mindset.

Growth Mindset and Extremism

I know people who got upset at me in college for not being liberal enough who now get upset at me for not being a hardcore conservative like them. They all say the same thing, "I used to be a liberal, but now I've transformed, and I see the truth!"

"Bitch...you were an asshole back when you were a liberal, and you remain the same asshole now."

Belief transformations mean nothing to me. The beliefs change, the core character remains the same. The need to impose those beliefs remains the same. The inability to see a different perspective remains the same. The toxic black-and-white thinking remains the same. They painted over a broken house when they should have torn it down and rebuilt it.

Now a mindset transformation from a fixed mindset to a growth mindset? That, I applaud.

In a mindset transformation, the beliefs may not change that much. But the person's relationship with those beliefs is much healthier.

Extremism is less about beliefs and more about people's relationships with those beliefs. Extremists from every extreme have a very similar toxic relationship with their beliefs.

Element Seven: Social Competence

The Significance of Social Competence

What's the point of grey area thinking if we cannot help our fellow humans? It will be very difficult to help people if we suck with people.

Regardless if you are an introvert or an extrovert, it's important to develop good social habits. Bad social habits will lead to a lot of closed doors.

In the age of smartphones, people won't bother to give you feedback. They'll just smile and quietly shut the door. If enough doors close on you, you'll be stuck with all the people everyone else closed their doors on.

Some people are there because they are difficult. Others are there because they are monsters. Don't be the difficult person stuck with monsters.

Besides, grey area thinking is best suited for complex social problems. I didn't exactly mention engineering problems in this book (seriously, make sure AI understands grey area thinking, so it doesn't kill us all).

If we are going to tackle issues such as the loneliness epidemic (which extremists take advantage of), we are going to need to be good with people.

The Significance of Social Competence

You don't need to be cool or charismatic. But you do need the fundamentals.

The fundamentals:
1. Be a safe person and make others feel safe.
2. Be able to form, recognize, and respect boundaries.
3. Emotional regulation and impulse control.
4. Appropriately connect with others.
5. Do not be clingy or needy.
6. Read social cues and recognize discomfort.
7. Be able to read the room.
8. Be self-sufficient and do not overburden others.

If you are a man and you are weird and difficult, I highly recommend focusing on becoming proficient at these skills instead of buying shit online to teach you how to talk to girls.

Just like any art or sport, no one cares about your fancy moves if your fundamentals suck.

Element Eight: Information Literacy

Information Literacy and Extremism

This section may offend... I don't give a fuck anymore.

Grey area thinking cannot replace quality information. However, in the age of misinformation, not everyone agrees on the best place to get quality information.

Today, there are conspiracy theories floating around claiming that western governments, higher education, and mainstream experts and media have been completely corrupted by "deep state" agendas. The "deep state" is a secret group of elites who want to control the world. Over a third of Americans believe in these theories.

I'm just going to rip the band-aid right off. *So, why don't you ever hear the world's smartest people talking about this?*

Every piece of conspiracy theory research available to the public can be seen by Harvard students and professionals from cognitively-intense fields, such as medicine and law.

I'm not trying to be an asshole, but the fact is, if you take 100 random "deep state" conspiracy theorists and 100 random Harvard kids, and they compete in 100 random intellectual contests, the Harvard kids will **outperform** in most battles. So, why don't the Harvard kids reach the same conclusions from the same conspiracy research?

"Because they are brainwashed!"

Perhaps. But then you realize that dictators throughout history, across every culture, mass-murdered elite scholars when they rose to power. Explain why Hitler, Stalin, Mao, Qin Shihuang, and Pol Pot burned books and hunted down intellectuals like dogs.

Chinese university students helped Mao Zedong to power. As soon as he got it, he betrayed them all. Why?

Because elite intellectuals are less likely to *stay* brainwashed. They can *get* brainwashed, but they don't *stay* brainwashed.

Yes, even the smartest people can fall for stupid things. But once the emotions wear off, they start to *self-reflect*. The greatest minds are full of doubt. Doubt leads to self-reflection. By contrast, the dumbest are full of confidence. They self-reflect a hell of a lot less. Therefore, they are easier to brainwash.

So, if you are the leader of the "deep state"—some shadow force out to control the world—why waste your energy brainwashing such a small part of the population whose allegiance is so hard to control?

Why not use the method proven to work over and over and over again? Brainwash everyone else. Then, get them to hunt down and kill all the hated nerds. Maybe that's the real conspiracy that's happening.

How to Get Quality Information?

Regardless of whether conspiracies exist or not, I believe there is a golden rule we can all follow when it comes to getting quality information.

To get the best information, seek out the largest number of the most excellent people. Then, understand what their limits are.

Why not just tell people to listen to the experts?

While I don't believe in conspiracy theories, I do believe that telling people to blindly follow the experts can lead to abuse or disaster.

First, good luck telling people to put all their faith in people they don't understand or trust.

Second, not every expert is the same. Some fields have weaker experts. Some experts come from regime states. Some experts follow outdated ways of thinking. Some experts make mistakes.

This is a big one: some experts fall under the spell of groupthink. NASA scientists made very avoidable mistakes that blew up the Challenger Space Shuttle in 1986. Many scientists knew something was wrong, but nobody wanted to be the loser who stopped the launch. Peer pressure made them silent.

By **contrast**, the collective wisdom of the largest number of the world's smartest people is greater than any one group of experts.

Regardless of how much corruption and brainwashing there is in the world, you can always place *some* faith in excellence. Excellence can be measured objectively. A simple contest can determine who deserves it.

Corruption and brainwashing can compromise individual and group excellence. However, that problem is solved with numbers. As a collective, large numbers of the world's smartest people spread *across* the globe are the least likely to be corrupted and the least likely to be wrong.

So let global excellence tell you which experts to listen to and what information to believe in. If indeed the experts are wrong or part of some conspiracy, the excellent will be the best people to investigate.

I will let you decide who you consider to be the "most excellent." Personally, I keep things simple. My list consists of:

1. Graduate students from the top 100 ranked universities
2. Top 5% performers of every industry

The Significance of Information Literacy

After you have created your "world's smartest" list, you have to understand its limits. The world's smartest humans are still human.

Let's examine the limits of the people on my list.

Graduate students from the top 50 ranked universities

Students are young, and young people do reckless things—even the smart ones. They often conform to toxic intellectual trends of the time. Chinese and Iranian college students helped Mao Zedong and Ayatollah Khomeini to power.

Today, fanatical progressivism is the reason why the public has lost faith in the credibility of higher education. Students and faculty who criticize progressivism face ostracization and harassment. Because of this, universities may withhold research funding for non-progressive topics.

Top 5% performers of every industry

Not everyone who deserves to be a top 5% performer is recognized. Twenty years ago, when Dr. Bennet Omalu was researching the link between American football and brain damage, experts of the time mocked him. He even received death threats from hardcore football fans.

Likewise, Charles Darwin (father of evolution) and Louis Pasteur (father of modern medicine) also faced intense opposition at the beginning of their careers.

Okay. Now that I understand the limits, I apply the grey area principle of **emphasis** to determine how limiting those limits actually are. College students follow reckless trends. So on issues that spark fanaticism, I remove fanatic students from my list. However, I don't jump to the conclusion that they are all brainwashed and useless.

If needed, I use the principle of **variety** to diversify my sources. If US college students get too political, then I can always look at what students from Singapore and Finland are saying.

I keep my mind open to the deserving but unrecognized performers. However, I apply the principle of **contrast** to make sure I don't waste time on people who seek attention by saying controversial things.

In the past, upstarts, such as Omalu, Darwin, and Pasteur, faced intense peer criticism in the beginning. However, once their work was made public, the scientific community reviewed it. A few short years later, their criticism stopped. New champions were crowned.

The key difference is *time*. Therefore, once information becomes public, and the more time that passes without its recognition, the less likely I'm going to believe it.

The Artist's Memoir

This is the final act of my book. Here, I share with my audience the events of my life that inspired the Art of Grey Area Thinking. The short stories run for multiple pages, so this is denser than earlier parts of the book.

Remember, I write this book primarily as an artist, not as an intellectual. In order to fully express my art, I will be raw. I will be unhinged.

I will curse a lot. I will criticize both the far-left and the far-right. As a liberal, I will be more vicious toward other liberals because I want us to be better. The Art of Grey Area Thinking is about self-reflection. The world does not need another liberal being nasty to conservatives. It needs self-criticism. I hope conservatives who read this can take inspiration and do the same.

If you are not comfortable, no hard feelings. To readers who continue, I am a flawed person. I hope to inspire the next grey area writer to be better.

Welcome to the fucking show.

Why Fighters Vote Right

In my senior year of high school, I wrestled varsity. There was this one tournament where I was not performing well.

I finally found my rhythm during a later match and began dominating my opponent. I was comfortably ahead by a significant margin of points.

Ten seconds remained on the clock, and my opponent was nearly scoreless.

Then, in a blind spot the referee could not see, my opponent grabbed my headgear and twisted it across my face. Taking advantage of my surprise, he threw me onto the mat and pinned me.

I tried to tell the referee, but my protest fell on deaf ears.

Livid was an understatement. I went berserk. I was pounding the floor like a rabid chimpanzee, screaming for a fight.

My teammate's father, Mr. Gammage, an accomplished wrestler in his youth, grabbed me and dragged me into the locker rooms.

Mr. Gammage was a no-nonsense African-American man, who came from a proud black family positioned firmly on the political left.

Mr. Gammage stoically waited while I blew off steam, crying, punching lockers, and screaming how the cheater wouldn't stand a chance if I also wrestled dirty.

Then coldly, without a shred of sympathy, Mr. Gammage said, "Then you should have finished him before he could do that."

"I'm the better man, and he knows it!" I said.

"Oh, yeah? You sure act like it." Mr. Gammage replied sarcastically.

Today, conservatives enjoy talking about resilience and personal responsibility. But I learned those values from liberals.

One of my biggest frustrations with my fellow liberals is that when we are legitimately criticized, we respond with, "But the Republicans did this or that."

Aren't we supposed to be better? And if they are as bad as we say they are, why the hell would we expect them to play fair?

Combat athletes are taught to make no excuses. We are expected to take criticism from our coaches and leave our egos at the door. Even when our opponents win unfairly, we ask, "What could we have done better?"

To be blunt, can anyone expect people with these values to respect progressives who automatically deflect criticism by bringing up the far-right?

To clear things up, warriors throughout history tended to be more conservative. However, at no point in modern history has it been this lopsided. Today, the near totality of the global Mixed Martial Arts community votes conservative. Just five years before, some of the most popular figures in MMA, such as the commentator Joe Rogan, were outspoken liberals.

In the event of a civil war, the entire liberal warrior class will consist of a handful of black athletes, that one trans-Navy Seal, and myself. Joking aside, if anyone thinks liberals do not need warriors, simply take a look at Ukraine and Iran.

Besides actual combat, warriors possess three essential values that are grey area thinking elements: courage, self-reflection, and a growth mindset.

No, you don't have to be a warrior to have these values—and not every single warrior has these values—however, the intensity of combat generally forces people to develop these traits to elite levels.

In order to write Art of Grey Area Thinking, I needed courage to confront difficult truths. I needed courage to write things that would

probably get me death threats from six different groups of people.

I needed self-reflection to eliminate my own bullshit, so I didn't give it to my readers. I needed a growth mindset to overcome my own vulnerability to manipulation and abuse.

So, when there is a mass exodus of warriors from the left, combat isn't the only thing that's leaving.

Liberals are losing people who do the right thing when it is hard. They are losing people who spent their entire lives accumulating wisdom from intense hardship and competition. They are losing creative problem solvers who never give up.

Most importantly, they are losing people who know how to get shit done.

All warriors care about performance.

(Tangent: Several beta readers commented that this line is black and white. I could have edited it to "most warriors care about performance," but I decided on a teaching moment. Grey area thinking criticizes _toxic_ black-and-white thinking. Not all black-and-white thinking is bad.)

Anyway, all warriors care about performance...what the fuck was I going to say again?

All warriors...care...performance...performance...all warriors care...oh yes.

So a few years ago, I was training in Jiujitsu in a very liberal Californian region called Silicon Valley. Sanitation is incredibly important to Jiujitsu gyms. Skin diseases such as staph infections and ringworms spread like wildfire.

Immediately showering after practice is mandatory. Surprisingly, not one Jiujitsu gym I visited in Silicon Valley had showers. This was incredibly weird and alarming.

When I asked gym owners why, they replied, "There's a law in this city: any gym that installs showers must install showers for disabled people. We simply don't have the space or money to do that."

I asked, "Is this enforced?"

"Occasionally, we get people that come into the gym with wheelchairs. They don't want to join. They don't know anybody in the gym. We're not even sure if they are actually disabled. They just roll around checking if the gym meets city standards for wheelchair accessibility. They are looking for a reason to sue."

While wheelchair-bound jiujitsu athletes do exist, they are incredibly rare. By forcing jiujitsu gyms to conform to these shower laws, the city was needlessly putting thousands of athletes at risk of painful skin infections.

Skin infections are a collective threat. The fewer people shower, the higher the risk for everyone. It is far safer to ask the rare disabled athlete to shower at home rather than to force everyone to shower at home.

Jiujitsu gyms were forced to make dangerous sacrifices because liberal officials wanted everyone to be more inclusive.

Liberals in America have a reputation as kind-hearted idealists who are terrible at executing those ideals. Their policies have good intentions but often make people's lives harder.

When liberals are criticized, they smugly defend liberal ideals and attack conservative flaws. They shove theories down people's throats and get pissed when they gag.

However, moderate Americans aren't criticizing the ideals. They are criticizing results.

If liberals want to perform better, then more liberals need to adopt a warrior's performance-based mindset.

Focus on results. Not just the results you are looking for. Listen to people whose lives were made harder by liberal policies. Amend those policies so you can be truly inclusive to more people.

That, and fewer people will hate us.

(This is the kind of precision grey area thinkers must develop—<u>problem-solving precision.</u> You get problem-solving precision through constant reflection and adjustment. You don't always have to be precise with your words.)

Thucydides, the greatest Ancient Greek Historian, said, "A nation that makes a great distinction between its scholars and its warriors will have its thinking done by cowards and its fighting done by fools."

Liberals call conservatives ignorant, while conservatives call liberals snowflakes. American college graduates are overwhelmingly liberal, while American warriors are overwhelmingly conservative. Of all the polarizations that could exist, the polarization of intellectuals against warriors is the one I find most frightening.

Liberals need to get their warriors back. We need to correct this imbalance. We can start by listening to our criticisms without compulsively blurting out, "But the Republicans did this or that!"

The Nightmare Before Cancel Culture

Halloween 2013. The last Halloween before the American far-left exploded with popularity.

I was a senior at UC Santa Barbara. Some Delta Gamma sorority girls invited me to a fraternity party at the Sigma Alpha Epsilon house.

For my non-American readers, fraternities and sororities are exclusive organizations attached to American universities. They organize lavish parties for members and their guests. Each university has about two dozen fraternity and sorority houses. Each house is named after Greek letters.

At my university, Sigma Alpha Epsilon had built a nasty reputation for bullying, hazing, and racism. But I wasn't going to say no to a bunch of Delta Gamma girls.

My group consisted of five DG girls, my friend Ian (white and brother of the DG girl who invited me), and an Asian-American named Alec. I am also Asian-American. Alec and I did not know each other.

I criticize the far-left a lot. But I'm not going to act like I never benefited from them. Before the woke movement (when far-left politics went viral amongst US millennials and generation Z), I heard racial slurs every other weekend at college. There was very little I could do.

Fighting was pointless. There was always the next asshole. I would get stabbed, arrested, or sued long before I put a dent in racism. Besides, party hosts were mostly concerned about aggression. I wouldn't be invited anywhere.

To make matters worse, around that time, there was a string of incidents where drunken white fraternity brothers would ambush and assault random Asian-American students on weekend nights.

This is exactly what happened that night to Alec at the Sigma Alpha Epsilon Halloween party.

A drunken SAE named Jackal randomly sucker-punched Alec. There was no warning, no provocation, and no inciting incident.

Alec and Jackal began fighting. Although I was not friends with Alec, we came from the same group. I had to help him.

Brawling was a bad idea. We only had three men. SAE had at least twenty brothers at that party. We were also in their frat house. Any of them could have pulled a weapon and claimed self-defense.

The DG girls rushed in to protect Alec while I grabbed Jackal and pinned him against the wall. I still remember the way he looked at me with his drunken wild eyes and sadistic grin.

A DG girl rushed over and convinced Jackal to calm down. Then, she escorted me out of the SAE house.

After I exited the front gate, I turned to wait for the rest of my friends when a curly-haired SAE brother, who resembled Viserys Targaryen from Game of Thrones, told me to get lost. (Daenerys' brother. The one killed by Khal Drogo.)

I told him I wasn't going anywhere without all my friends. I demanded to know why they attacked us. He replied, demanding to know why we were in his house in the first place.

"Some Delta Gamma girls invited us."

"Who?"

"M."

"Then, I don't care. M doesn't suck my dick."

I grew up in a locker room. I have heard worse. My friends have said worse. But it wasn't what he said. It was the way he said it. It was that tone. So matter-of-fact. His voice felt empty of humanity.

Ian, M's older brother, was the last to emerge from the gate. On his way out, some SAE brothers heckled him relentlessly. Finally, when Ian was nearly at the gate, he'd had enough.

Two SAE brothers got too close for comfort, and Ian threw a punch.

They were both bigger than Ian. It wasn't a fair fight... for SAE. Ian whooped their asses!

Panic quickly covered Viserys' face, and he squealed, "Call the cops! Call the cops!"

I could not help but fantasize about burying a Viking axe into that frat boy's skull over and over and over again.

Power. That's what triggered me. First, the power behind his tone when he said, "*M doesn't suck my dick,*" and then the power he had when he squealed, "*Call the cops.*"

Power this despicable, dishonorable, spineless filth neither earned nor deserved—power he used to abuse others and escape accountability.

However, his power would not last.

In 2014, far-left movements swept across US college campuses like a tsunami. Students began shaming people who made racist comments or sexually harassed women. They boycotted businesses that employed them, forcing their managers to fire them.

Cancel culture had been born. And, as a minority, it seemed like racism disappeared overnight. We no longer had to fight.
We could just pull out our phones, hit record, and the racists would lose their jobs.

Hollywood began firing film executives who sexually harassed actresses. Powerful men who got away with rape in the 1980s and 1990s were finally sentenced for their crimes. The bullies who attacked LGBT people were now the ones being hunted.

With the help of cancel culture, disadvantaged people now had the power to fight back.

But it came at a cost.

Once the far-left gained full control of liberal culture, things would take a nasty turn.

At first, cancel culture was doing its job. The left focused on putting rapists in jail and racists out of work.

But then, the far-left started canceling people who made an honest mistake and said something slightly offensive. Petty, but whatever.

Then suddenly, all conservatives were automatically racist. Uh...grapefruit? (Grapefruit is my safe word.)

Cancel culture started with the intention of holding people accountable. But it became a witch-hunt and lost its original purpose.

Like the traffic cop who ignores the Ferrari speeding 100 mph to go after the sucker driving 75 in a 65, the cancel mob abandoned their pursuit against truly despicable people to send death threats to JK fucking Rowling.

JK Rowling, the author of the Harry Potter books, made several comments on her Twitter expressing minor frustrations regarding transgender bathroom policies and cultural issues surrounding gender identity.

She did so gently, using no offensive language. She didn't even criticize transgender people. She only criticized their zealous activists.

For over two years, far-left Twitter users harassed Rowling with tens of thousands of hate messages. Every time I read Rowling's Twitter, I had to double-check if she got away with murder.

And every single time, I wonder which nightmare I prefer: the Halloween I spent with those deplorable frat boys or watching the far-left try to 'help' us minorities.

I am still a liberal because I truly believe that we have the right core values. However, my experience with the far-left's cancel culture taught me that core values are not enough.

This revelation inspired my belief that grey area thinkers should not only strive to do the right thing but also in the right way, for the right reasons, and in the right amount. When we violate the grey area principle of scale, we self-sabotage, regardless if we are right.

When people criticize liberals for cancel culture, liberals usually respond with, "But the conservatives also cancel."

Yes, the conservatives also "cancel." They ban books. They criticize black athletes who kneel to protest police brutality during the National Anthem at sporting events. They harass abortion doctors and transgender activists.

So why is the world more upset with liberal cancel culture? Because conservatives are *supposed* to cancel! They've been doing it for thousands of years. They are *supposed* to be less tolerant and less inclusive.

By contrast, tolerance is a classic liberal core value. Yes, there are limits to our tolerance, as there should be, but our limits are supposed to be further than the conservatives. Yet, we are pettier, more hostile, and more easily offended (grey area principles: contrast, emphasis, scale).

When conservatives cancel, at least they do so with a sense of proportion. Thousands of conservatives do not harass black athletes years after an incident.

They have their outburst and move the fuck on.

By contrast, in late 2022, JK Rowling was still receiving hundreds of hate messages a day from the left for minor comments she made in 2020.

By violating the grey area principle of scale, liberals betrayed their tolerance value. People are less upset with conservatives because they never had the value to betray in the first place.

The principle of performance in the Art of Grey Area Thinking teaches us that having the right idea is not enough. You have to execute that idea and then track its progress so you can make adjustments.

As a liberal minority, I have not had a single white far-leftist come up to me and ask, "How are we doing? Is this what you guys wanted? Are we doing a good job?"

I would tell them that this isn't what most of us wanted. I would tell them that it feels cringy and inauthentic when they do the whole "Oh, you poor baby minority, white people must be purified by fire" act.

Instead, I have white far-leftists explode on me for disagreeing with them on minority issues. As soon as you disagree with them, they stop seeing you as human. They don't care who you are.

They don't care about what you've done to help the world. All they care about is the disagreement.

People who do that tell me they don't really care about helping minorities. They care about their egos. It leads me to wonder: was social justice, this whole time, more about the white middle-class kid's search for meaning?

Because if it was truly about minorities, why the fuck didn't they ask us how they were doing?

Intellectual Bully

In 2016, I was walking in a park with my friend Bee from college. Bee has a Ph.D. in math. He is a cognitive powerhouse.

We discussed my experience living abroad in the Middle East. We eventually landed on the topic of misogyny and how women are treated.

Politically, Bee, a white male, was far-left. He was not keen on hearing any minority group portrayed in a negative light.

By contrast, I am a minority. I grew up playing mostly with Middle Eastern friends. I have lived in Turkey and have a nuanced and respectful understanding of their culture.

So when I made a casual remark that the Middle East had more misogyny than the United States, Bee was not happy. He demanded evidence.

I told him about the stories of domestic abuse and honor killings I had heard about.

He replied, "That's anecdotal experience. Your personal experiences do not count."

I offered a compromise. I met a Turkish woman experiencing workplace misogyny who was treated poorly by her family. I emotionally supported her through social media.

She wanted more westerners to hear about what she was going through. I offered to show Bee our messages.

He replied, "No, that's still anecdotal evidence. You need to give me empirical data."

"Bee, we are walking in a fucking park. I'm not going to Google empirical research on my fucking phone. Can we just move on?"

No.

"Fine, what's your empirical evidence that the United States is more misogynistic than the Middle East?"

I fucking kid you not. Bee, the math Ph.D., one of the smartest people I knew, said, "In World War II, we dropped atomic bombs on Japan. Those bombs killed a lot of women. So because we killed more women, we are more misogynistic."

Years later, when I returned to Turkey, I told a female grad student about this conversation. She practically screamed at him through me, "He wants empirical evidence? I'll fucking give him empirical evidence."

My walk In the park with Bee taught me that even very intelligent people can be irrational. I am confident that my friend knows the difference between war casualties and ongoing practices that solely harm women.

But in the moment, Bee had to win the argument. Bee had allowed himself to be swallowed up by the fanatical far-left movements sweeping across American college campuses. In these movements, minorities must never be criticized (unless they disagree with the far-left).

Thus, emotional intelligence is a crucial element of grey area thinking because emotions affect thoughts. We can get swept up by emotions no matter how smart we are. This is especially true when we join groups and lose our individuality. Group emotions overtake the individual mind.

This goes for the far-left, the far-right, and the far-fuck (far-fuck is whatever you want it to be).

If we lose emotional balance, we also lose a balanced perspective. Because Bee couldn't create healthy boundaries against his need to be right, he couldn't form boundaries between academics and a casual walk in the park. Hence, he made a very unreasonable demand for evidence when I said something that was common knowledge (a violation of the unity principle: making unreasonable demands).

Because Bee couldn't create healthy boundaries for his individuality, he couldn't stop his politics from overtaking his reason. Hence, he couldn't allow himself to think anything negative about minorities.

As grey area thinkers, we can stop group emotions from overtaking us by creating strong internal boundaries. We can join groups to serve a greater good, but the group can't touch what belongs to us: our autonomy and reason.

With some groups, you have to give up part of yourself to be with the group (like the military), but you can't give up your whole self. However, in those groups, the lines between autonomy, duty, and loyalty become blurred. Therefore, you must adjust continuously for more precise boundaries to avoid losing your balance.

One of the elements of grey area thinking is information literacy. We need to know the difference between the good shit and the horse shit. Under that section in the book, I urged my readers to trust the largest number of the world's smartest people.

Unfortunately, a lot of really smart people are fucking things up right now.

Highly educated people need to understand that the world can't afford them to be intellectual bullies.

The world needs its smartest people to guide the rest of us.

If someone is willfully ignorant, put them in their place. But don't go around dominating people who aren't even trying to compete with you.

Part of the reason why misinformation and wild conspiracy theories are so popular today is that many people have lost faith in our elite institutions. My walk in the park with Bee isn't a unique incident. You can find countless students online sharing similar stories of elite scholars trying to bully fellow students into far-left politics.

I feel it is important for grey area thinkers to know how to defend themselves against an intellectual bully. Today, a very common intellectual bullying tactic is what Bee did, an unnecessary demand for empirical evidence (violation of the unity principle).

But first, it's essential to know what empirical evidence is. Peer-reviewed empirical evidence is information that has gone through the highest available quality assurance process.

Think of it as a piece of gold that has been melted over and over again. What's left is then dissolved in acid and filtered for gold particles. That process is repeated by many different goldsmiths until you get 24 Karat gold. That is called peer-reviewed empirical evidence.

During a formal intellectual discussion, people who offer personal experience (officially known as anecdotal evidence) should generally yield to people who present empirical evidence.

However, that doesn't mean empirical evidence is omniscient.

Gold purification is expensive. Empirical research is also expensive. Therefore, empirical evidence isn't available for everything. Just like how not every piece of gold gets to be 24 Karats.

Thus, it's okay to sometimes use peasant 23-karat gold. Likewise, in a casual conversation, it's okay to fill in the blanks with weaker evidence.

As long as you acknowledge the limitations of your anecdotes, you can use them. The wrong way to go about it is to say, "My experience is the only thing that matters." But most people who use anecdotes don't mean it that way.

If you feel you are reasonably using anecdotes, but an academic bully says you can't, you fight for your voice to belong.

"I understand the limitations of anecdotes. However, human beings have been exchanging knowledge with anecdotes for millions of years. If you have a specific problem with my anecdote or how I am using it, please tell me. If I make a mistake, I will correct it. Otherwise, you don't have a right to silence me."

If you need something quicker, use: "Explain why my anecdote is such a threat."

Fighting unreasonable demands is a strategy from the grey area principle of unity. You can apply this strategy against a wide variety of intellectual bullying tactics, such as when someone raises the difficulty of their vocabulary or asks for unnecessary details.

If empirical evidence is 24 Karat gold, then jewelry is the argument. Jewelry stores don't sell you a lump of gold particles. A jeweler has to craft that gold into something people can wear.

Likewise, someone who brings empirical evidence into a debate still needs to pair that evidence with good reasoning. When intellectuals are desperate to win an argument, they often mess this up.

Like my friend Bee, they overreach with the evidence. You can then exploit that overreach with a good comeback. But first, determine what the overreach is. Here are some common overreaches:

1. The scope of empirical studies is usually very narrow. The conclusion of that study might not justify the argument your opponent is making.

2. The study's research might not have collected the correct information for the argument.

3. Your opponent doesn't know jackshit about the study.

The last one is especially important. Unless it's your responsibility to "do the research," you don't have to do it.

You are a busy person. If someone is trying to convince you not to use your anecdote, *they* need to convince *you*. Therefore, the burden is on them to answer basic questions about the research.

"I just want to make sure that your research applies to your argument. Because I know you respect my time, I'm sure you won't mind answering some basic questions about the research you brought up. You were talking about the US being more misogynistic than the Middle East.

Your evidence is Japanese World War II casualties. Misogyny is about the intentional discrimination of women. Can you confirm that your evidence concludes that the US bombed Japan to harm women discriminately?"

There are several grey area principles in play. First, the principle of emphasis. I use the overreach of my opponent's argument against him like a Judo throw. I repeat his words back to him and show him how irrelevant they are. Second, I practiced the principle of contrast by clearly defining the difference between misogyny and war casualties.

The difference was discrimination. Discrimination is the link that justifies the removal of Bee's evidence from the debate. As you guys know, unity is also about eliminating things that don't belong.

Notice how the principles of grey area thinking intertwine and work together. Emphasis reveals irrelevance, and contrast reveals key differences. Both help unity eliminate what doesn't belong (it's been far too long since I said fuck).

Reversely, not every demand for empirical evidence in a non-academic conversation is unreasonable. If you are making an extraordinary claim, it's your responsibility to back it up with whatever people need.

If you are making a claim that can truly affect someone's life (for example, their health), then it is your responsibility to give them whatever evidence they want.

Notice how the emphasis always comes back to responsibility? If you are presenting anecdotal evidence, you have to ask yourself if you're doing it responsibly.

Reversely, if you present empirical evidence, you also have to do it responsibly. You need to actually understand the study. You need to read the room to see if that evidence is required. You don't just throw it out there and expect people to submit.

Lastly, I hope that the academics reading this can learn to stop relying on empirical evidence in every situation. It's your job to deal with the empirical. Not everyone else's.

If that's the only thing you have, you will be incredibly limited when communicating with people. There is a time when empirical evidence does not belong. There is a time for anecdotes, storytelling, and casual conversation.

And if you can't understand that, the public will continue to ignore you and choose misinformation.

Escaping a Cult

In the summer of 2013, I joined a cult.

I was working in the film industry in Los Angeles, and I needed a way to move up in that cesspool. So I aggressively sought out networking opportunities, film classes, and seminars. And I did so, completely broke.

There is no one easier to manipulate than the desperate and the ambitious. I was both. I joined the cult so I could have access to its low-cost film events.

Of course, to qualify for those film events, I also had to attend the cult's self-improvement classes, which was essentially their indoctrination process. They put you in a room with 20 other recruits and a supervisor who provides you with cult reading material.

At that point in my life, I was highly vulnerable to emotional manipulation. I was a lost kid searching for meaning. I was incredibly naïve and easily trusting. I did not understand how to protect my boundaries. I did not understand power and the nasty things people did for it.

I was the perfect target. Except, I paid attention in school.

"Communication 88, Research Methods in Social Science" was a boring, tedious, and difficult class. However, it was the most important class I ever took at UC Santa Barbara. It saved my ass from that cult.

It taught me the difference between good social science and shit social science. I intuitively recognized the shit from the cult's self-improvement classes. I saw past the flawed logic, and the crude attempts to use statistics.

Red sirens blaring inside my head, I recalled another lesson from my school reading: how Hitler brainwashed the German people during his early rise to power. It was almost as if the cult took that textbook and applied those methods step by step.

I saw how the cult's roused leader worship just as the Germans had. I saw the cult subtly encourage blind allegiance while suggesting that all its critics were evil. I saw the cult gradually isolate its members from outside influences such as family and friends.

"I have to go to the bathroom."

I took the elevator down to the ground floor and said I needed some fresh air. As soon as I was outside the cathedral (yeah... they had a cathedral...with fucking elevators), I sprinted to the bus stop and never looked back.

Sometimes, I wonder what happened to the other 20 people in that class. Probably now all sex slaves or some shit.

I wrote this book for people sitting in that class right now.

I wrote it for the people standing on the edge of the vortex but haven't yet jumped in. Once people jump in, they'll fight the people trying to pull them out.

Cults get us through the door by playing on our hopes and fears. But they keep us there by controlling our self-esteem.

I knew about this cult's reputation before I joined. There were many stories online about them swindling people for money.

The first cult employee I spoke with was an Asian girl who spoke accented English. She seemed so completely normal that I let down my guard. She even joked, "check your pockets," when I told her I read online that her organization "takes people's money."

She convinced me to be open-minded. Later that week, despite being broke, I paid them several hundred dollars.

Human beings struggle with sunk costs. When we make bad decisions, we are inclined to rationalize those decisions to protect our egos.

In 1950, a middle-aged American woman named Marian Keech was convinced she was receiving messages from outer space. She convinced a small but loyal group of followers that the Earth would be destroyed by a great flood. However, aliens would come with spaceships to rescue her and her followers.

According to Keech, their alien saviors were supposed to arrive at midnight on December 21, 1950. At 4:45 am, Keech addressed her highly anxious followers. "The aliens told me they flaked on us because the Earth isn't being destroyed after all. We impressed God with our faith so much that He decided to spare Earth."

Keech's followers had quit their jobs and given up most of their possessions. They dumped her body into... no, they didn't. That would have made some fucking sense.

No. Keech's followers erupted in wild cheers. They became even more fanatical followers of their leader. Keech and her crew had avoided media attention before. But after that revelation, they spoke to every reporter they could find. Conviction is one hell of a drug.

Self-reflection is an essential grey area element because it teaches us to accept sunk costs. Having a healthy ego lets us learn from our mistakes instead of lying to ourselves about them. We cannot do the right thing if we are lying to ourselves.

A big reason why cults get people to give up money and possessions (either to the cult itself or to charity) is to get them to lie to themselves. The more people give, the more they give in. The higher the sunk costs, the lower people sink into self-deception.

The cult I joined in 2013 targets young actors. Young actors are broke as fuck. Los Angeles is expensive as fuck. So when we give away hundreds of dollars, it's hard to admit we got played. The cult uses that to trap actors into staying.

Luckily, my dumbass had already lost over a thousand dollars to pyramid schemes. It's easier to admit you've lost hundreds when you've already lost thousands. To break out of a cult's trap, we must be willing to let go. It's okay to make mistakes. *It's fucking okay...*

I must reiterate the importance of education in helping me escape the cult when I did. The better your education, the better your information literacy.

To my right is a book called "Age of Propaganda: The Everyday Use and Abuse of Persuasion" by Anthony Pratkanis and Elliot Aronson. Ten years ago, I was supposed to read this book for class. I only read half a chapter. By sheer luck, that was the chapter about brainwashing tactics. That was the chapter that helped me escape from the cult.

"Age of Propaganda" was published in the year 2000. Yet, this book contains highly detailed information about most of the issues we see today: cults, misinformation, political extremism, populists like Donald Trump, Russian state propaganda, etc. Very little of what we see today is new. Yet, society completely failed to apply the lessons in this book to stop those threats.

If you want to protect yourself from manipulation, you must educate yourself beyond the Art of Grey Area Thinking. In the long run, the more you learn, the better your chances. "Age of Propaganda" is a good continuation in that direction.

Virgin Mass Shooter

I was two blocks away when Elliot Rodger attempted to massacre the entire UC Santa Barbara Alpha Phi sorority house. I heard the shots that killed Katie Cooper, my dance teacher, who, by bad luck, just happened to be around the corner.

I remember smiling because I thought the popping noises were fireworks rather than gunshots. Fireworks were common in the party town of Isla Vista—a festive suburban ghetto that housed 20,000 UC Santa Barbara and Santa Barbara City College students within a square mile.

In 2014, UC Santa Barbara was considered the third biggest party school in the US. After the mass shooting of May 23, 2014, we were so sick of that title we wanted our entire party legacy gone.

For years leading up to the shooting, UC Santa Barbara had developed a highly exaggerated reputation for casual sex.

During my freshmen orientation, senior student volunteers worked really hard to try and dispel this myth. They showed us studies that the average UCSB student only had sex with one partner per year. They had chosen the best-looking volunteers to present this study.

Of course, it didn't matter. Who gives a shit about a study when there's a good story? We were students of UCSB, the University of Casual Sex and Beer. Besides, who wants to be average?

Here's the recipe. Thousands of young men, all living within a square mile, forced to prove their worth by conquering women in a pressure cooker environment that shamed men who couldn't. Exactly what do you expect to happen?

Well, for starters, every single man except me was having a threesome every other week. The stories we tell ourselves are one hell of a drug. Especially stories that hide shame.

Shame constructed by social pressures violates two grey principles: balance and unity.

Shame distorts reality. It replaces our true needs with false needs. Shame manufactures unnecessary self-conflict, creating destructive false beliefs.

We told exaggerated stories about our sexual exploits to hide our shame. Those stories came at a price.

Women walking home alone at night were dragged into the bushes and raped by multiple men. Unsuspecting female foreign exchange students were lured into houses and barred from leaving. It would be harder to find someone who didn't have a female friend who was raped.

Things became so dangerous for women that when I said hi to a female friend and she couldn't recognize me because I had my sunglasses on, she immediately had a fight or flight reaction. This was in broad daylight.

A religious friend once told me, "We are like [the Biblical city] of Sodom." Except, we weren't Sodom. By this point, most of us were sick of excessive partying and all the bullshit it brought. But while we were exhausted with our reputation, the rest of the world wasn't.

Tens of thousands of out-of-towners, including gang members from all over California, flocked to our tiny college town to experience our infamous hook-up scene. When the promised land failed to deliver, which was the most likely outcome, they took out their frustrations by destroying our homes and cars and robbing and assaulting students.

Many of these out-of-towners decide to stay. They signed up for classes at SBCC, a local community college, with no intention of ever taking them seriously. They were there for one thing: to get laid in a town filled with terrified and hostile women.

One of these boys was Elliot Rodger, son of Hollywood director Peter Rodger. He lived in Isla Vista for three years, trying his luck at losing his virginity. But, laden with severe mental illnesses and completely lacking in basic social skills, Rodger failed to garner any female affection, much less lose his virginity.

Rodger went online and joined misogynistic forums and far-right communities. There, he radicalized alongside fellow lonely men who believed that the source of all evil was that women would not sleep with them.

He was part of a group called PUA-hate, an extremist forum that hates both women and PUAs. PUAs, or pickup artists, are people who use rehearsed routines to seduce women. They make money by teaching other men their craft. Most of it is bullshit and doesn't work. However, socially challenged men will pay thousands of dollars to work with PUAs.

Taking a man who has never kissed a girl before and telling him that, within a few weeks of 'training,' he could become the next Hugh Hefner is like telling a man who has never run a mile before that he could become an elite athlete in the same amount of time.

It's very easy to figure out that a man has PUA training when they speak to women. It's so cringy, you would rather listen to nails on a chalkboard. I would know. I was a buyer.

What PUAs are really selling is false hope to men with low self-esteem. And when you sell hope, the buyers buy to believe. And the more people pay to believe, the more they self-deceive.

However, it's only a matter of time before the illusion shatters. Many PUAs are politically far-right. They will redirect their student's inevitable frustrations against modern women. Their fail-safe is to scapegoat feminism and the breakdown of traditional values.

Although I cannot confirm this, I can take an educated guess that this was Rodger's natural progression. Rodger likely got involved with one or more far-right PUA teachers, got swindled, and became resentful of PUAs but kept the misogyny.

Fueled with entitlement and frustration, Rodger lashed out. He started small, splashing coffee on girls who did not smile back at him. He escalated this behavior until, one day, he tried to shove a girl who rejected him over a ledge with a ten-foot drop.

Her male friends leaped into action, grabbing Rodger and throwing him over the ledge. Working as a journalist during the time of the shooting, I interviewed Rodger's neighbor, who saw him limp home that day, swearing to kill them all.

Say what you want about feminism, but no woman has ever picked up a gun and killed six innocent people because she couldn't get laid (... yet. In America, you never know).

I criticize extreme progressives, but I criticize with a sense of proportion. Hardcore feminists can't take a joke. At their worst, they may occasionally punish an innocent man for abuse or rape.

By contrast, hardcore misogynists join terrorist groups and slaughter innocent people. ISIS? Those were fucking Incels.

You cannot fairly criticize far-left fanaticism without understanding what they are fanatically running away from. They go too far because they don't ever want to go back.

I knew three of Rodger's victims. In total, he murdered six and wounded fifteen. But he didn't act alone. Thousands of men who refused to put boundaries on sex acted with him (grey area principle of balance).

The pickup artists who believe that sex is more important than honesty and compassion acted with Rodger. The Incels who felt entitled to sex acted with Rodger. The culture that told young men they were nothing unless they conquered women acted with Rodger.

Misogyny, combined with black-and-white thinking, led to the murder of my classmates. Rodger was just the tip of the iceberg.

Social competence is an element in grey area thinking because, ultimately, we have to share this world with other people. And if we want to do things right, we need to think with other humans in mind.

When people think about social competence, we usually think of coolness or charisma. However, there are things that matter a lot more.

First, there are social fundamentals. Young men who struggle socially shouldn't be learning how to pick up girls from online douchebags. A far better long-term investment would be to master basic social skills (direction: long-term). For example, self-awareness and how to appropriately connect with others.

Second, there's social responsibility. Being cool isn't always right. For us, it was cool to conquer women. But where did that lead us? Sometimes, it takes more social competence not to fit in.

Lastly, there's social awareness. The girls at my school were fucking terrified. If everybody had just paused, we would have realized that our school's reputation for sex was either highly exaggerated or no longer the case. We were willfully blind until it was too late.

The day after the mass shooting, almost every male in Isla Vista admitted that they rarely or never got laid. Some of the most popular men I knew told me they didn't lose their virginities until junior or senior year. Two weeks later, I graduated from the University of Casual Sex and Beer, a virgin. I was damn good-looking, and I partied hard.

And just like that, the Emperor had no clothes.

A New Way To Believe

In December 2016, I attempted suicide. It took all my willpower not to follow through. It felt like lifting an impossible weight.

Later that day, I was diagnosed with manic depression, more commonly known as Bipolar I. I would wake up laughing hysterically. Two hours later, I was crying. Then laughing again. Then back to crying. It was some Joker shit.

You know the expression, "the walls are closing in?" So for me, that was literal. And when I experienced that, I was like, "yeah, fuck this, I'm out." I just wanted it to end.

This isn't a mental health book, so I'll go with the short version: it was a very happy ending. By January 2018, after a year of hardship and dedicated recovery, I became depression free; all symptoms of mania were gone. By 2019, I stopped having mood swings completely.

The most important aspect of my recovery was Kundalini yoga, one of the harshest forms of yoga. It involves intense breathing, chanting, and painful endurance exercises. Without Kundalini, I would not have recovered.

In yoga, there's this belief called "chakras." They are basically these rainbow balls of psychic energy that line up from your butthole to the top of your head. Many yogis believe that when you practice yoga, you "align your chakras."

When aligned, chakras help people achieve spiritual insight and emotional healing.

The belief in chakras is a constant friction between yogis and scientists. Many yogis fanatically swear by it, and scientists fanatically make fun of it. My teacher took a different approach.

One day, after an exhausting kriya (intense breathing combined with torturous exercise), our teacher opened his eyes and said, "You guys know that chakras aren't real, right? They are figments of our imagination."

He smiled and winked at us, and then he closed his eyes, and we went back to doing more painful shit.

But at that moment, I knew. So many things began to make sense to me. My teacher had just helped me discover a powerful truth.

The belief itself does not matter. What matters is what you do with that belief.

Chakras are real in our minds. Realness and existence are two different things. As long as something is real in your mind, you can use it. It doesn't have to exist to be real (principle of contrast: knowing key differences).

Chakras are real because they have a powerful psychological effect on us. That psychological effect helped me beat Bipolar I without medication or therapy (I couldn't afford therapy. Please don't attempt this).

The argument between yogis and scientists about whether or not chakras exist physically is a waste of time. It doesn't matter. The more important thing is that chakras can work in our imagination to bring about positive change.

Humankind spends so much time fighting over beliefs while ignoring what they do with those beliefs. The important thing is the direction a belief takes someone.

Because Kundalini saved my life, from 2017 to 2020, I promoted that practice to anyone who would listen. I swore by it. I constantly posted about it. In my view, it was the best thing since sliced bread.

But then, in the summer of 2020, I read something terrible. Kundalini Yoga founder Yogi Bhajan, who died in 2004, was a cult leader (me and my fucking cults). Like Harvey Weinstein and Choudhury Bikram, founder of Bikram yoga, he sexually abused dozens of women.

As for the practice of Kundalini, an investigative report by UC Santa Barbara's religious studies department uncovered a terrible truth.

Yogi Bhajan, or Harbhajan Singh Khalsa, stole a bunch of techniques from other yoga disciplines, mixed them up, and pulled the rest out of his ass.

Bhajan claimed to be a Sikh master and said that Kundalini yoga was a thousand-year-old practice from the Sikh traditions. I have spoken to many Sikhs about him. No one knew who he was. No one knew what Kundalini was.

Kundalini yoga is a cult. Luckily for me, my Kundalini teacher was a good man who shielded me from the cult. He simply taught me the practice and left out the bullshit.

We both walked away from Kundalini, but it wasn't easy. I felt so confused, humiliated, and enraged by this revelation that I put a hole in my bathroom wall.

In truth, I was scared to death. I proudly told everyone I recovered miraculously from bipolar I without medicine and therapy.

Doctors warned me that I could experience dangerous relapses. "If something triggers you, it can all come rushing back like a tsunami."

I was terrified. What if Kundalini yoga was a placebo? What if, this whole time, it was the drug I used to replace actual medication?

Now that my belief in Kundalini has been shattered, what if that drug stops working?

Dark memories of 2016 flooded my mind.

"Fuck it. If it comes back, I'll beat it. I beat it once; I'll beat it again," I said, determined but terrified.

It never came back. Two years later, I remain without mood swings or any bipolar symptoms.

My belief in Kundalini worked, even though its origin story was complete bullshit.

The principle of unity is about getting the best of both worlds. In this case, I reaped all the benefits of bullshit while suffering none of its consequences. The world can be strange like that sometimes.

Many Kundalini practitioners were unable to follow in my footsteps. Blindly loyal to Yogi Bhajan, they rejected every accusation and viciously defended their leader.

"The practice has helped far too many people. It cannot be taken away!" They cried.

As I watched them struggle with the truth, I wanted to tear my heart out of my chest.

Kundalini saved my life.

I had already healed from my illness and no longer needed to believe in Kundalini. But what about the people who haven't healed yet? What if what happened to me in 2016 waited until 2020?

Then, a thought occurred to me. Is there another way I could look at this problem (principle of variety)?

I contacted Phillip Deslippe, the UC Santa Barbara religious historian who took down Yogi Bhajan. I thanked him for his work and told him my story.

Then I asked him if he could share with me which yoga teachers Yogi Bhajan stole his techniques from. Specifically, the "ego eradicator' pose that worked wonders to quell my mood swings.

Deslippe analyzed the Kundalini pose I sent him and replied, "I do not know the exact origins of "Ego Eradicator" (or many of the specific exercises), but it looks like it is combining elements from Swami Dev Murti and Swami Dhirendra (with the breathing and navel pumping)."

The answer gave me closure. I was relieved to hear that I was healed by legitimate breathing techniques even though they were plagiarized. I can share this information to help others. And if I ever did relapse, I have a place to go.

That day, I truly became a grey area thinker. Without knowing it, I combined the unity principle with the variety principle to reconcile two difficult and conflicting truths.

The following statements are true:

1. The founder of Kundalini yoga was a rapist, scam artist, and cult leader. His practice was completely fabricated.

2. That fabricated practice helped many people and saved my life. But, because of the truth, its capacity to help others is no longer the same.

I harmonized both statements by asking, "Is there another way to help others get the same quality help I received without Kundalini yoga?"

The reason I was able to do what many Kundalini practitioners could not was because of the lesson my teacher taught me about belief.

It's what you do with the belief that matters. We shouldn't take the belief itself too seriously.

The purpose of a belief isn't for us to grip it so tight that we feel threatened by nonbelievers. The purpose of a belief is to help us build character and achieve wonders.

We need to form healthy boundaries with our beliefs, so *we* control *them*, not the other way around. Ironically, people who are controlled by their beliefs often swing from extreme belief to the opposite extreme (principle of balance: imbalance from lack of boundaries).

Without balance, they accumulate unmet needs. Those unmet needs eventually make them ill. So out of desperation, they pendulum to meet those needs.

These are the people who were far-left extremists in college but then became far-right extremists in their mid-twenties. They are the former homophobes who became aggressively woke.

They are the religious extremists who used to bully religious people back when they were extreme atheists. They are the misogynists who studied feminism in college.

These transformations don't represent healthy growth because while they changed their beliefs, their beliefs didn't change their true character. They were assholes before their transformation, and they remain the same asshole after their transformation.

My journey with yoga spirituality taught me that character matters more than ideology. The founder of Kundalini yoga said all the right things, but in real life, he was a piece of shit.

Ukraine: Fog of War

Ukraine: Fighting Russian Propaganda

Ukraine Part One: The Fog of War

I first began writing the Art of Grey Area Thinking in January 2022. At the time, the problems I was addressing were exclusively first-world. Far-left-far-right drama. Cults. Pyramid schemes. Abusive hippy boyfriends. That kind of shit.

Then on February 24, 2022, Russia launched an unjustified military invasion of Ukraine. I was in the region, so I traveled to the Polish-Ukrainian border to volunteer as a humanitarian.

I thought I knew what grey area thinking was. I thought I was an expert on manipulation and abuse. I was about to get a fucking wake-up call.

On my first day volunteering at the Medyka refugee camp, I was approached by someone who I am now almost certain is a human trafficker. He asked me, "Who do I speak to give Ukrainian [women and children] rides to Italy?"

Luckily, I was briefed beforehand that if anybody approached me with this question, I was to answer, "The police."

If nobody had told me, I might have absent-mindedly gone around telling Ukrainians that this man was offering rides to Italy. He was incredibly charismatic. He didn't look like a bad guy. He reminded me of a coworker you are always happy to see.

If my suspicions are correct, that man had singled me out because he could tell I was new. There were dozens of other volunteers that were obviously more experienced and confident, but he chose me.

That was day one. Welcome to a refugee crisis.

While I was volunteering at Medyka, I put my journalism and film background to good use. I shot documentaries and interviewed humanitarians, refugees, and soldiers who traveled from all over the world to volunteer and fight for Ukraine.

On my last day of volunteering, I interviewed a man claiming to be part of the Dutch Special Forces. It was raining hard. About a dozen volunteers and I had been huddled around the fireplace at the volunteer's rest and recreation tent.

A chubby man in military gear stumbled in, asking for assistance. He was Dutch Special Forces, and he had just returned from Ukraine. When he tried to volunteer for the Ukrainian Foreign Legion, the Ukrainians tortured him out of paranoia, thinking he might be a Russian spy.

I brought him food and filmed an interview with him. The next day, I received a call from a fellow volunteer who had experience with the Ukrainian Foreign Legion.

The 'Dutch man' I interviewed had been caught with a Russian SIM card in his phone. Furthermore, he had been going around collecting personal information on other soldiers. We immediately contacted the Polish army and police, but he was gone.

In hindsight, the Russian saboteur's story was ridiculous to begin with. He was Special Forces, yet he couldn't even keep up with me on a jog across camp. He fought in Afghanistan and was briefly captured by the Taliban but escaped. Oh, and he needed money to get back to Holland.

But guess what? I, and many others, believed him. I, the "expert" on manipulation, believed him. We believed him because he had audacity.

Because of his audacity, I started playing games with my own mind. He may be chubby, but who am I to judge? Maybe he was bullied for being chubby, and he used that as motivation to become Special Forces. He couldn't keep up with me on a jog—but, hey, maybe he was an excellent sharpshooter?

Audacity is a highly effective deception tool because most human beings are capable of telling the occasional small lie. Occasionally, we might tell a big lie. However, most of us aren't capable of telling big lies all the time.

Because we naturally assume that other people have our psychological and moral limits, audacious liars blow past our defenses.

Hence, audacity is a mass manipulation method favored by both Russian propagandists and western far-right populists. In the face of bold lie after bold lie, the people's resistance crumbles. No one can possibly lie that often.

As soon as people fall under that spell, they don't want to climb out. Because to climb out, they have to admit that they **got played**. And that's too big of a blow to their ego.

It's okay to admit that you got swindled. What matters more is that you have the strength of character to admit that someone got the better of you. It's more important to come back than it is to never be manipulated.

I walked into Medyka thinking I was an expert on beating manipulation. I had a lifetime of experience dealing with bullies, cults, and abusive people. I had spent over a hundred hours researching and reading about manipulation and abuse.

Yet, at Medyka, I was easily swindled.

If admitting that makes my readers doubt my ability to teach them about anti-manipulation, then good. The biggest danger for my readers is that they walk away from this book thinking they are invincible. Because if you think you are too good to be manipulated, you won't admit it if you *do* get manipulated.

Some of the best and the worst people show up at warzones. I made lifelong friends volunteering at Medyka. I also dealt with human traffickers, Russian saboteurs, and scam artists posing as humanitarians. One of the most popular humanitarians at Medyka during the time I was there turned out to be a conman.

I worked alongside some of the best people I've ever met. Yet I could not fully trust everyone I befriended. They couldn't fully trust me either. Misinformation was mixed in with good information.

Soldiers call that kind of warzone ambiguity: the fog of war. And the fog of war is as grey as they come.

Perhaps the biggest lesson I learned from the fog of war was the importance of grey area thinking elements.

I had to find balance within my emotions. The dangers required me to be vigilant, but if I was going to be useful, I couldn't afford to become paranoid.

I had to be courageous. If I were a pushover, bad people would take advantage of me. Stressed-out good people would accuse me of things I did not do. I had to stand up for myself, but I needed to do so in a way that was proportionate (principle of scale: proportion).

I had to know when to be silent. If I gave the wrong person too much information, I could bring harm to others. Furthermore, quieting my mind allowed me to listen and observe.

Information was essential to helping me avoid manipulation and danger. Ultimately, information is what feeds every principle of grey area thinking.

Character was important. A strong character naturally separates you from bad company. In a warzone, you can't afford to be wrapped up with the wrong people.

Social intelligence allowed me to create a vast network of friends across camp. A diverse network of friends is a wide safety net. If one friend turns out to be a conman or a Russian saboteur, you have other friends to support you. A diverse network of friends is also a diverse network of information.

In the fog of war, the last thing you want is to be isolated to one information source. A larger social network gives you a variety of insights, perspectives, and intel.

In my early drafts of the Art of Grey Thinking, I prioritized the principles. In fact, I didn't even have elements to begin with. Instead, the elements were simply a code of conduct because I didn't want assholes using my work to hurt people.

However, when I reflect upon my experience as a wartime humanitarian, I realize that the higher the stakes rose, the more I came to rely upon the elements. Ultimately, those elements are what allow us to use the principles of grey area thinking to the best of our ability.

Ukraine Part II: Fighting Russian Propaganda

After I returned home from Ukraine, I went online to fight Russian propaganda. I published Youtube documentaries of Ukrainian refugees who shared stories that directly contradicted the Kremlin's propaganda narratives.

Sometimes, I engaged Russian propagandists in the comment sections of various social media platforms. It was in these conflicts where I first witnessed the abusive party criticize black-and-white thinking to justify their actions.

Russians and their western sympathizers would tell people that there were both sides of the story. And if you only talk about Russian atrocities, then you are thinking in black and white.

Simply criticizing black-and-white thinking doesn't make anybody a grey area thinker. Simply because you look at both sides doesn't make you a grey area thinker. It's not enough.

Grey area thinking follows the principle of scale. Numbers matter. People who ignore numbers when they criticize black-and-white thinking are using black-and-white thinking.

The severity of Russian war crimes and corruption vastly exceeds Ukraine's. When one side is clearly worse, but you treat them the same, you are using toxic black-and-white thinking.

Volume suppression is a tactic used by abusive parties to gaslight everyone into forgetting that differences in severity exist.

Putin's propagandists and sympathizers frequently use one Ukrainian war crime to cancel out far more and far worse Russian war crimes. Furthermore, it is very common for Russian propagandists to bring up past US war crimes to justify their invasion on the global stage.

Again, there is a vast difference between the overall humanity and ethics of the US military and the Russian military. Russian propagandists try to erase those differences because when everyone is just as bad, then no one is.

When someone wrongfully criticizes you for using black-and-white thinking, defend yourself using the principle of scale. You cannot be a black-and-white thinker if you think in the right proportions.

That being said, you still shouldn't defend any party using black-and-white thinking. One of the biggest mistakes I see Americans make when fighting Russia propaganda is when they pretend Ukraine is pristine.

No one is perfect. If you put the people you defend on impossible pedestals, then you are making it very easy for the aggressor to knock them down.

In the summer of 2022, a far-right influencer posted a video on Instagram bragging about how she outsmarted a New York Times journalist.

If she is telling the truth, the New York Times journalist had sent her an email demanding to know why the influencer called Ukraine corrupt in some of her previous videos.

The journalist stated that her views are similar to those that appear on Russia's propaganda websites, implying that she is a paid Russian propagandist (which she could be).

The influencer messaged back with links to several articles written by New York Times in the past about corruption in Ukraine. To millions of viewers, the influencer gloated that the journalist could do nothing but thank her for the links, but she was sure that the journalist had "died a little on the inside."

If that story is true, then that kind of humiliation is unacceptable. By using black-and-white thinking to defend Ukraine, the journalist helped humiliate Ukraine.

In life, humiliation is inevitable. We have to risk humiliation if we want to grow. However, if we don't take steps to prevent needless humiliation, then we are irresponsible. And if we are not willing to be responsible, we shouldn't be the ones talking.

With a little more prudence, the journalist could have avoided needless humiliation. To take things further, if the journalist combined the grey area principles of scale and unity, they could have easily won the argument. Imagine if the journalist had messaged the influencer with the following mindset:

"Just like how most countries in the world struggle with corruption, Ukraine is no exception. There are certainly things that can and should be improved. However, Ukrainians do not deserve to be unjustly invaded because they struggle with corruption. Making "no corruption" a criterion for US aid is a highly unreasonable demand."

Moving forward, I imagine that more and more people are going to start criticizing black-and-white thinking. The public is tired of black-and-white thinking. However, toxic black-and-white thinkers can also join the bandwagon and criticize black-and-white thinking.

Remember, manipulative people often project their flaws onto other people. They will twist words. They will corrupt ideals. They will exploit the truth.

It's not enough to criticize black-and-white thinking. By studying the principles carefully, you can go beyond that. When you yourself are faced with a narcissist accusing you of black-and-white thinking when you are not, you will stand strong because you have grey area principles.

Future of the Greys

2600 years ago, in ancient China, there lived a very wise man. He worked as a librarian for the Zhou Dynasty's Imperial Library.

As he was getting ready to retire, people begged him to write down his wisdom in a book.

Nope.

Then the last day of work came, and he prepared to leave forever. So a guard stuck a spear in his face and said, "The fuck you ain't until you write some shit down... sir."

Exact words.

Thus, Lao Tzu had no choice but to publish the Dao De Jing, or the Way of the Dao. Then he rode off on a buffalo, never to be seen again.

Some Daoist scholars believe that Lao Tzu was reluctant to write a book because he found written language far too limiting. He did not wish to be worshipped. He did not wish to be responsible for people twisting his philosophy to justify weird and terrible things.

Therefore, unlike Confucius, Lao Tzu made his book brief, ambiguous, and poetically cryptic. His wisdom was supposed to be slippery and elusive. If the reader isn't truly ready to understand an entire passage, then it is better for the reader not to understand at all.

That way, the reader cannot make half-truths out of his knowledge.

All of Lao Tzu's fears come true anyway. Lao Tzu was deified. Superstitious Chinese concocted mystical stories about his origins. People twisted his words and used them out of context.

Numerous Daoist cults sprang up throughout Chinese history. They persist even today. Some were incredibly destructive. For example, the Yellow Turban Rebellion in 184 AD, which led to millions dead, was led by a Dao cultist. While the rebellion itself was justified, I'm sure Lao Tzu did not appreciate them name-dropping him.

At this time, I have no idea how successful the Art of Grey Thinking will be. However, I know that if I am lucky enough to be successful, Grey will inevitably suffer the same fate as every other piece of inspiring writing. It will be misquoted, taken out of context, and used in fucked-up ways that I would never approve of.

In 2016, Chess Champion Gary Kasparov tweeted: "The point of modern propaganda isn't only to misinform or push an agenda. It is to exhaust your critical thinking, to annihilate truth."

Kasparov was criticizing far-right conspiracy theorists and Russian propaganda. Today, you can find that quote circulating amongst social media accounts that post far-right conspiracy theories and Russian propaganda.

Part of me hopes that happens to The Art of Grey Area Thinking because if it doesn't, that means this book wasn't successful. However, the rest of me really isn't looking forward to that.

The only assurance I have that my ideas will not one day be used to justify mass murders, cults, and unforeseeable destruction is you.

If my work has touched you, I hope that you use the principles of The Art of Grey Area Thinking responsibly. It is in your hands now.

I hope you share it with others. But I hope you don't shove it down their throats.

I hope you can reach people I can't reach. I hope you can reach an audience who dislikes my tone, my writing style, and my creative choices.

I hope you can write your own grey area book using empirical evidence to satisfy the nerds who refuse to read mine.

I hope you can write your own grey area book using a persuasive and gentle tone to help save the people I chose to fight (because they sure as hell need saving from my readers... just kidding).

I hope you merge my work with other disciplines. I hope to see it merge with science, politics, technology, business, art, and medicine to help humanity accomplish wonders.

I hope to see grey area thinking design the products I use (c'mon, tech companies; minimalism doesn't count for shit if our favorite features are removed).

I hope you build upon my work, adapting it to the times and refining the art with your knowledge and creativity.

I hope you apply these principles to help combat the greatest threats of your generation and make the world a better place.

Lastly, I hope you use the Art of Grey Area Thinking with love.

Artist: Nadif Abdelhak and Ulyana Dikhtyar

The End

References:

Fifty Shades of... who the hell reads the references anyways? Just use this page for extra workspace.